Canadian Cataloguing in Publication Data
Bachelder, Thomas
    You made this?! : a guide to making wine no
one knows is homemade

ISBN 0-919571-16-6

    1. Wine and wine making – Amateurs' manuals
I.   Title.

TP548.2.B33   1992   641.8'72   C92-090474-2

Typeset in CG Omega
Cover in Gill Sans
Typesetting: Willow Young-Codner

Kylix Media Inc.
Montréal, Canada 1992

You MADE This?!

A Guide to Making Wine No One Knows is Homemade

by Thomas Bachelder

Cover Design: Linda Connors
Cover Photo: Russell Proulx
Illustrations: Sharron Leggett

PUBLISHED BY KYLIX MEDIA INC.

† *"So thy barns be filled with plenty
and thy presses burst with new wine."*

Proverbs 3:10

† *"Wine is a living study, a lifelong study,
capable of infinite variations of thought,
knowledge and subtle experience with the palate,
the eye, the nose and the mind...*

*Therefore, anything which extends the wine lover's
knowledge of his (or her) subject is in itself good.
He (she) cannot learn too much about wine; the
tragedy is that he will learn too little in his span...*

*So many things go into the handling of wine, more
in fact than go into any other drink or food, that a
continual opening of the mind about wine cannot
but further the appreciation of it."*

David Gunston, *Wine Tidings* Magazine 106, October 1987

† *"I have lived temperately, eating little animal food.
Vegetables constitute my principal diet.
I double, however, the doctor's glass and a half
of wine, and even treble it with a friend."*

Thomas Jefferson

† *"How simple and frugal a thing is happiness –
A glass of wine, a roast chestnut, a wretched little
brazier, the sound of the sea."*

Nikos Kazantzakis 1883-1957

Table of Contents

An Encouragement

Pathetic Beginnings: How I Started

It is an interesting comment on our society that the average person thinks winemaking beyond her or his capability. For several millennia, winemaking has been a part of every European family's autumn routine: in effect, everyone was a home winemaker! Of course, back then everyone was a baker, cook, fashion designer, singer and farmer, too!

High-Tech, High-Touch

We can't go back to those days – nor would it be desirable, but in a high-tech time when actors act for us, singers sing for us, and food and clothing is made for us, making wine is the perfect "high-touch" activity to re-establish a tie with this earth of ours, with our ancestors who led useful, fulfilling lives toiling and tilling the land.

1

People regard home winemakers with a mixture of awe and distrust, as if we were some sort of weird, mystical alchemists wielding unnaturally-acquired powers beyond the scope of the average mortal. Well, perhaps that's going a bit far, but the truth is, I was as scared of making wine as anyone. The difference is, I wasn't afraid to try!

Making wine is no harder than baking bread or putting in a garden and the rewards are just as great. If you love wine, you may just love making wine: the thrill of making a portion of your yearly wine needs, the aspect of being a little tied to the seasons is wonderful. While others bemoan the quick passing of summer, you'll look to the fall with renewed hope....

Home winemaking is more popular than ever before, and for good reason! While commercial wines continue to climb in price, the cost of making wine at home has remained more or less stable and the chances of producing a decent, drinkable wine are better than ever.

For many, (this writer included) the "Holy Grail" of home winemaking is the pursuit of that elusive wine that no-one knows is homemade...the wine that the self-styled "connoisseur" down the block fails to pick out in a batch of medium-quality French (or Italian, or American, or Canadian) wines.

For others, however, the thrill lies in the "back-to-the-earth" sense of satisfaction they derive from making and drinking their own wine, while yet others find that the money saving aspect of winemaking affords them the option of having an inexhaustible supply of wine for everyday consumption at their fingertips. Instead of drinking a more expensive commercial wine of often questionable quality, they find they can grace their table with a bottle of "Chateau Chez-moi" at least twice as often as they could otherwise afford to.

Whatever your persuasion, rest assured that "You MADE This?!" will ease you into the joys of home winemaking. Whether you hope to make a Château Latour clone, or just something to throw in the Boeuf Bourguignon, the rules are the same for all...follow our basic instructions, get into the swing of it, and the sky's the limit!

In a few years, you may find yourself searching for that "missing link" adjunct which will give your concentrate wine that "extra something," or, perhaps come October, you'll be at the railroad siding or market – or a local vineyard - pinching and tasting the freshly imported grapes with the experienced eye of an old pro. Whatever your involvement, you will have personally plumbed the depths of the question that has fascinated man since time immemorial: How does grape juice turn into wine? Like making a photograph come to life in a darkroom tray for the first time, you will turn sweet juice into glorious-tasting dry wine despite the ribbing, non-encouragement, and dire predictions heaped upon you by not-so-well meaning family and friends.

I believe winemaking in North America is big these days because wine has become important, become a part of Everyperson's lifestyle. An entire continent has rediscovered the joys of drinking wine after years of submission to the influence of the twin spectres of Puritanism and Prohibition.

North Americans make wine because it's fun; because it's a healthful and exciting way of filling their spare time; because it gives them something to dream about, to talk about; because they want to save money; because they want to get "back to the earth"; because they want to try to make wine that is better than much of the commercial plonk; because they want to provide wine for their extended family and friends; because they want to avoid the commercial overuse of sulphite and other additives; and some just make wine for the pure thrill of the chase!

Not surprisingly, there are as many ways to make wine as there are reasons for making it! Making wine can be very simple or very difficult; at its most basic, it's a time-honoured story of grape juice and yeast, an age-old story where the grapes call the tune and the winemaker drinks whatever results. At the other end of the spectrum, winemaking can be an incredibly involved procedure, for it is possible to control every step of the operation. It's up to you to choose where you fit in the grey area between these two extremes, between art and science.

If I Can Make Wine, Anyone Can!

One Christmas, there was a very strange shaped package under the tree from my brother, home for the holidays from university. Inside, there was a one quart can of concentrate to make "Beaujolais-type" wine, along with a pail, a gallon plastic container, an airlock, sheet of plastic and a siphon – that's all.

Could it really be that easy? I was hooked before even reading the instructions! That kit made 6 bottles of wine (1 Imperial Gallon), and I have never looked back! (Well, except, perhaps for that batch of "Burgundy" that went "off," oh, and that sulphide-y and sulphite-y batch of "Médoc!")

I can still remember how I wrote down a friend's "Doubting Thomas" remarks: "This will never work!" "You can't make wine in a cupboard!" "You're adding sugar? – It's going to taste like Port!" Needless to say, her remarks made my giddy success seem all the more phenomenal, and in the end she became a willing convert.

The simple, nay, miraculous fermentation of grape juice into wine has never ceased to rouse wonder in my heart, and one look at a vat of seething, hissing, frothing, outrageously purple wine fermenting is enough to quicken my pulse; the writing of these very words makes me long for the autumn ritual!

This book was written not for experts, but for the laywomen and men who need a gentle push... an encouragement to discover the joys of making wine from the "holy blood of the grape," as Hemingway called it.

There are many things to remember when making wine, it is true, but what nobody tells you is that many of them are obvious, and come naturally (like the proverbial bike ride) after a few times. You won't find any chemical equations in this tome, but you will find the do's and don'ts, the special secret-yet-simple tips ("Cellar Hints") passed hand to hand through a thousand generations of winemaking.

Get your hands dirty. Evolve your own preferred ways of working, set your own goals. Listen to constructive criticism of other people who like wine. Serve your wine in a previously-emptied commercial bottle and get the real reaction. Challenge yourself and your palate: compare your product against commercial wines. Don't be too hasty: let your wine age before and after you bottle it: taste it at its best. (You drank commercial wine before, you can drink it while you're waiting). And remember, tasting is the best way to improve.

I hope I've removed some of the barriers for you. It's up to you to take the initiative to embark on what can be an enjoyable, life-affirming and life-long avocation!

Take the leap of faith, join with us making wine; become proud of your links with the soil, with the seasonal cycles, and the weather; become a winemaker and join the sister and brotherhood that has been making wine that has gladdened the hearts of man since time immemorial. Most of all remember, no matter what any snob, disbeliever or "Doubting Thomas" says – you are not just a home winemaker, you are a WINEMAKER!

Thomas Bachelder
July 1992

Section I

Why Don't You Make Wine?
...For Those Who Never Thought They'd Make Wine

A Note From the Author:

The aim of *You Made This?* is to give the aspiring and intermediate winemaker the concrete, practical "how-to's" of making wine in small quantities at home. A conscious decision has been made to avoid the overly technical, and concentrate on providing the reader with an enjoyable, encouraging, friendly first manual on making wine at home.

If, someday, the reader moves on to more technical texts in search of a greater understanding of the scientific principles that govern winemaking, this little book will have served its purpose just as equally as if that day never comes, and *You Made This?* remains the main text referred to as the winemaker stockpiles her or his own knowledge.

Why Grapes?

Those who love drinking and making fruit wines may be perturbed to find little mention made of them in this book. That is because I believe – although I have made and tasted delicious fruit wines – the study of grape wines to be the most important.

Grapes are the ONLY fruit that naturally ferments into wine all on its own – all the winemaker basically provides is control: cleanliness and protection from oxidation. Grapes are born with their own "4-Week Wine Kit!" – the necessary sugar, tannin, acid, water, nutrients (and even yeasts on the skin!) to become wine, one of the most complex and hedonistic pleasures this life provides!

NOTE: For fruit wines see the Bibliography for Pattie Vargas' and Rich Gulling's excellent new book called "Country Wines," which is easy to read and chock-full of recipes.

How To Use This Book!

Although the book has been arranged in separate "chronological" sections (in the natural sequence of winemaking), the reader might first read the section on her or his area of interest (concentrates, juices, or fresh grapes) proceeding to the "general interest" chapters.

As an example, those interested in making wine from, say, juice, would read the Fermentation Fundamentals section, skip the Concentrate and Grape sections, and then proceed to the last third of the book. The General Wine Techniques; Wine Maturation; Bottling and Labelling; Cellaring; Other Techniques; World of Wine and Wine Disorder sections apply more or less equally to ALL winemakers.

Readers who want to keep making concentrates (as an example), but want to learn some "A-level" tips should read through the sections on winemaking from fresh grapes, which are chock-full of winemaking tips and tidbits, some of which may apply to the way you make concentrates.

A Note On Metric vs. U.S.
vs Imperial Measurement Systems

When temperatures and volumes are referred to in this text, I have tried to give two equivalents, where possible. Thus, what is a 19 litre carboy to me will have the equivalent (five gallons U.S.) in brackets. What is a 50 gallon oak barrel to me may be a 225 litre barrique to you. In places where measurement is not critical, I have rounded off the figures, so you aren't adding, say 23.46 grams of sulphite to water to make a sulphite solution for sterilizing equipment.

I have stayed away from giving exact measuring instructions when it comes to using commercial products like acid test kits and fining agents. These products are made by many different manufacturers, so it is best you understand the concept from the book, then apply it to the particular product you have bought, following that manufacturer's instructions.

Illustrations

Sharron Leggett's artistic, beautifully-executed pen and ink-drawings are the perfect synthesis between practical technicality and being aesthetically pleasing to look at. Partly the result of the author reading too many winemaking books that would illustrate only the equipment, and not HOW the actual equipment is used, Sharron has attempted, both through the drawings and their rather long captions, to illustrate, demystify and convey a feeling for the very physical mechanics of the major aspects of successful winemaking.

Glossary

ASSEMBLAGE: A blend of similar, complementary grape types with a view to creating a wine that is greater than the sum of its parts.

AIRLOCK: See "Fermentation Lock."

AROMA: Primary grape fragrance in young wine or must that disappears as the wine ages.

ASTRINGENCY: The component of a wine (due to tannin) that causes the mouth to pucker.

BALLING: See °BRIX.

BARREL, BARRIQUE or CASK AGING: When a wine that is fermented in a primary vessel or vat (of cement, plastic, glass, stainless steel, epoxy or open-topped wood) is subsequently matured in a small white oak (usually French, American or Slovenian) cask of 225L (50 gallon) or less, we refer to this as "Barrel Aging."

BARREL-FERMENTED: A wine (usually white) is said to be "Barrel-Fermented" when it is actually fermented (after pressing and removal of skins) in a 225L (50 gallon) or less, usually new oak barrel.

BODY: The "Mouthfeel," the full, round feeling that some wines have (or lack) in the mouth.

BOUQUET: The more complex fragrance that arises with the aging of wine, as the aroma dissipates.

°BRIX (Degrees Brix): The percentage of dissolved solids in a must, and since most of the dissolved solids in must are sugar, °Brix is equal to or slightly more than the percentage of sugar. °BALLING are, for our purposes, the same as Brix.

BLOOM: The whitish deposit, or thin film, on a grape at maturity containing yeasts, moulds and bacteria.

CAP or CHAPEAU: The hard mass of grape skins that are forced to the top of the fermenting vat during fermentation.

CHAI: The fermenting room and/or wine maturation room of a winery.

CHAPTALISATION: Adding sugar to a must before fermentation to increase the potential alcohol content. First suggested by French doctor J. Chaptal, for stabilizing the low-alcohol wines made from unripe grapes.

CLONE: A vine reproduced by cuttings taken from the parent. A clone will be genetically-identical to the parent, unless it mutates.

COOPER: A barrel maker.

CROSS: A crossing is the offspring of two parent vines within the same species, i.e., Vinifera. See "HYBRID."

CRUSH: Before the fermentation occurs, the grapes must be put through a crusher, or carefully squeezed by hand into the primary fermenter, to lightly break the skins and allow some of the juice to run out.

CUVÉE: Wine kept in separate and distinct lots, as in: "We put this cuvée of Chardonnay in new French oak for three months, while this other cuvée spent six months in two-year old American barrels."

EXTRACT: Sometimes referred to as "sugar-free extract;" consists of various minerals and non-volatile matter found in wine. Wines with high extract levels are generally more mouthfilling, and come, usually from riper grapes. Wines from less ripe grapes or over-productive vines will have less extract, and, consequently, less perceived value.

FERMENTER: A container or vat (usually open on top) in which the beginnings of fermentation take place.

FERMENTATION LOCK: A device which, filled with water or a sulphite solution, permits CO_2 bubbles to rise out of a container of fermenting wine without letting any air in. Placed in a bung with a hole in it, the whole unit is then placed in the neck of the carboy, or the bung hole of the barrel.

FINING: Adding a substance to wine to remove cloudiness as it falls to the bottom of the container.

HERBACEOUSNESS: In wine, a vegetal, herb-influenced taste or bouquet. Can be positive, adding to complexity, or not, depending on the degree.

HYBRID: The offspring of two parent vines of different species, i.e., Vinifera X Riparia. See "CROSS."

HYDROGEN SULPHIDE: An acrid rotten egg smell produced from certain types of yeasts in interaction with wine, usually occurring when the wine has been left too long on the gross lees. Racking may lessen but will rarely completely correct the problem.

LEES: Sediment, or deposit on the bottom of the container of fermenting or finished wine. Usually contains spent yeast, grape solids and other compounds.

LUG, or CASE: A 36 lb. (16 kilogram) wooden box made specifically for the shipping of grapes. (Great for storing Bordeaux bottles, too: see the "Cellar Hint" in the "Bottling and Labelling" section.)

MOUSSEUX: French term for sparkling wine made outside the region of Champagne, "PÉTILLANT" is also used.

MOUTHFEEL: See "BODY"

MUST: ready to ferment, unfermented grape juice (may contain skins and stems or not) until the time it starts fermenting.

OXIDATION: The chemical changes, (some of which benefit a wine, and others which do not) that occur with wine's exposure to air.

PIPETTE: See "Wine Thief."

PITCH THE YEAST – means either simply sprinkling the dry yeast on the surface of the must OR pouring a prepared yeast starter into the must. To prepare a starter, the dried yeast is added to a small quantity of fresh must – about a litre. When it is fermenting rapidly, add this starter to the larger bulk of fermenting must.

PLONK: A simple, table wine with no geographical origin, except perhaps its country of origin. A blended wine that offends no one, but has no real complexity or character of its own. While

11

"Plonk" is often used in a derogatory way, it can also be used with a bit of affection: "This is a great little glass of plonk for the price; I could drink this every night!"

POMACE: What is left of the grapeskins after they have been pressed.

PUNCHING DOWN: The act of pushing the hard cap of skins back into the fermenting must. These skins are forced to the top of the vat by the release of CO_2, much the same way that the release of CO_2 makes bread rise. Exposed grape skins are not protected by the alcohol of the madly fermenting wine, so they must be pushed under the surface of the wine at least twice daily. As well, "Punching Down" helps to extract colour, body, tannin, taste and aroma compounds from the grape skins.

PUNT: The indented heel of some heavier wine bottles, originally intended to make it easier to store vast quantities of bottles, tucking the neck of one into the punt of the other. Today, bottles with punts are prized for their ability to collect sediment when stood up a day or two before serving. Generally, the more expensive wines will be put up in punted bottles.

RACKING: To rack is to siphon wine from an elevated container (on a table) to a container on the floor. This is done to separate the wine from its lees, to aerate the young wine and allow it to clear itself naturally. One also siphons a wine to bottle it, but this is not called racking.

RECONSTITUTED MUST: Like reconstituted orange juice, reconstituted must is concentrated grape juice that has been brought back to its original volume by the addition of water (and sometimes sugar, acid and tannin). Correctly reconstituted must can be considered, for the purposes of fermentation, as grape juice.

SEDIMENT: See "LEES."

SIPHON: A long, clear plastic hose used to transfer wine from one container to another. See also "RACKING."

STRUCTURE: The body, acids, tannin and astringency of a wine. One could think of structure as the "posture" of wine's "BODY".

SULPHITE: POTASSIUM METABISULFITE VS. SODIUM BISULPHATE: two white powders prized by winemakers for their sterilizing and anti-oxidant qualities. Various sulphurs have been used by winemakers for hundreds and hundreds of years, usually in the form of burning sulphur wicks.

STUCK FERMENTATION: A fermentation that has stopped while there is still an undesirable quantity of sugar left in the must.

TABLE WINE: A wine that is of the ideal alcohol level (generally considered between 10.5-13 per cent), flavour and body to harmonize well with dinner. Historically, table wines have been considered the beverage of moderation. There are simple table wines, and great, breathtaking table wines.

TANNIN: An astringent component of wine, derived from the skins, stalks and pips of the grape. Gives colour and improves the keeping quality of wines.

TENTURIER: Grapes with coloured pulp (juice) as well as coloured skins, used for blending with lighter-coloured grapes.

TERROIR: A unique combination of aspect (placement of vineyard), climate and subsoil minerals that the French feel give definition and complexity to their best wines. The Californians have only recently publicly admitted there may be some truth to what was originally seen as French chauvinism for their own products.

TOPPING UP: Keeping a vessel of wine full so that there is a minimum of airspace between the wine and the closure, to avoid airborne bacterial problems and oxidation.

TRIAGE: The selection or sorting through of grapes after they are picked, but just before they enter the crusher. Stray leaves are pulled out, and unripe, mouldy, rotten or otherwise imperfect grapes are eliminated or set aside to keep them from lessening the quality of the "Grand Vin."

WINE THIEF: A long cylinder whose sides are so thin that it can be submerged in a narrow-necked container or barrel without causing the wine to overflow. Once the Wine Thief has slowly submerged at its own speed, the thumb is applied to the small opening at the top and the Wine Thief (now full of wine) may be drawn out of the container, and poured into a tasting glass.

VINEGAR: Alcohol that has been transformed into acetic acid by oxidation, and exposure to the Acetobacter bacteria.

VINTAGE: The wine produced in a given year.

VITICULTURE: The growing of the grapevine.

Section II

Fermentation Fundamentals (for all wine styles)

Basic Equipment

Equipment is a non-problem – really! All you need for basic winemaking from juice or concentrate are the barest essentials. To make a five gallon (19 litre) batch of wine (26 750ml bottles!), you'll need a siphon hose, a primary fermenter, and a carboy for your secondary fermenter. Most wine stores have a starter "special" that will include these items and more (excluding the juice) for about $50, (or perhaps less, depending on your resourcefulness) but many "hooked" winemakers soon avail themselves of every useful time and labour-saving device on the market!

This same basic equipment can be used to make wines from concentrates, fresh and pasteurized juices, and even for beermaking. Wine from fresh grapes requires additional capital investment, but this equipment can be added as the need arises, keeping your original equipment as the nucleus of your "system."

Whether you live in an urban centre or in the wild, there is a winemaker's supply store (check yellow pages) within striking distance. Many stores also do a brisk mail-order business, however, it's fun to browse and ask questions of the staff — universally known for their helpfulness.

Depending on your involvement, the acquisition of additional equipment can be inexpensive or quite expensive, like so many of the finer things in life.

So here, in checklist form, is what you'll need to get a start on making wine from concentrates or grape juice:
– a primary fermenter (food grade plastic bucket)
– a sheet of plastic to cover the bucket, with cord and elastic
– a hydrometer and a floating thermometer
– a siphon
– a secondary fermenter fitted with an airlock. This is a five U.S. gallon (19 litre) carboy, or the 5 imperial gallon (23 litre) carboy, but the 20 litre carboy is also becoming popular.
NOTE: *For the purposes of simplicity, throughout the book, the author has referred to the 19 litre, five gallon size carboy. Please adapt this to your carboy size.*
– concentrate or juice: your choice of the popular "bag-in-box" complete with sugar (5 litre-100 oz.); traditional concentrate (one gallon-4.5 litre); or grape juice (five gallons-20 litres).
– yeast
– Sugar (for some concentrates only)
– Sulphite (Metabisulphite)
– oak chips (optional)
– 26 clean bottles
– bottle corker and corks
– labels and plastic capsules.

The **primary fermenter** is simply a plastic bucket. This is the container into which the reconstituted (or whole) juice is first

Fig. 1a

A piece of cord and a strong elastic band can serve to tie down the plastic sheet.

Fig. 1b

The plastic primary fermenter must be covered during fermentation. A towel or sheet will work, but a plastic sheet is better. Before using, rinse the plastic and spray it with sulphite solution to sterilize it. Then, tie down the sheet using a cord and an elastic band (Fig. 1a), or join two bungie cords together.

poured. It must be fairly unscratched inside, be of food-grade (usually white) plastic, and have a capacity of just over 5 gallons (19 litres). Although you will be making a five gallon batch, the must does froth up in the early stages of fermentation, and a too-small container can lead to loss and infection. A primary fermenter can be had quite cheaply at your local winemaker's supply store, or you can try to obtain a used vegetable oil bucket free from a local restaurant. Beware of buckets which have held chemicals, for scratches can harbour nasties!

The **plastic sheet** is the device which covers your must from the time you pitch your yeast until you siphon, or rack, the young wine into the secondary fermenter. It should be large enough to have 15 inches or so (40 cm) overhang on all sides so that it can be tied to the bucket. (Fig. 1b, p. 17)

| *Cellar Hint:* | **TYING THE PLASTIC SHEET DOWN** |

It's a good trick to cut a piece of cord about the same size as the circumference of the bucket, and then tie each end to the two "ends" of a strong rubber band. In this way, you will be assured of both a snug fit, without having to constantly re-tie a cord, and an easily-removable lid. "Bungie Cords," those large cloth-covered elastic cords with hooks on the end, are also great for the purpose. Hook two together, if need be. (Fig. 1a)

The **floating thermometer** is not an absolute necessity, but it sure makes it easy to "pitch the yeast!" (inoculate the must). Yeast is quite particular about the temperature at which it will function, and you will find the thermometer a real yeast-saver! An equally-important function of the thermometer is to monitor the temperature of fermentation, so that the must does not experience wild temperature swings.

The **hydrometer** is a floating weighted glass tube which measures the density of liquids in relation to water; necessary for knowing sugar content, final alcohol content, and, most importantly, when fermentation is finished. See the Section on "How to Overcome Your Fear of Hydrometers."

The **siphon** is used for transferring your wine from the 1st to the 2nd fermenter, and to get the wine into the bottles. Special spring-loaded stopper ends are available for this purpose.

The **carboy**, or **secondary fermenter** is most often a 19 litre glass carboy which can be purchased from your wine supply store, or from wherever you can find them still full of spring water, which is their original *raison d'être*. You will need a **fermentation lock** (which lets air out but not in) and a **rubber bung** to plug the carboy's neck. You may also purchase a handle for the carboy at your winemaker's store, and I am certain you will want one immediately after lifting your filled carboy for the first time! The glass carboys are much preferable to the new plastic ones, which may impart a plasticky taste to your wine.

Metabisulphite or **sulphite** is an all purpose chemical which inhibits the growth of wild yeast and other nasties, cleans equipment, and prevents wine from oxidizing too quickly. Yes, this is the stuff from the salad bar scares, but it's in all commercial wines, especially those not bottled at source. It's a necessary evil, and one that you can judiciously control.

Oak chips are dropped into the secondary fermenter to give the wine a taste of "oak barrel". Wine made this way takes a little longer to be drinkable, but with superior end results. See Section 8 for a detailed look at the "How-To."

Bottles can be saved, cleaned, and stripped of their labels by you, or bought for a nominal sum at your supply store. See Section 9.

The **bottle corker** can be bought or rented from your local supply store. They come in a range of sizes, styles, and prices starting at about $15. See Section 9.

Corks are very important if you plan to keep your wine for any time at all. Inferior quality corks crumble, are hard to insert, and could be bad for your precious wine. Spend the buck or two extra per 100; get the extra long, pure corks (not the "pressed-cork" amalgamations), and sleep at night! See Section 9.

Labels and **Capsules** are completely frivolous, having nothing to do with the quality of the finished wine, but they look great! Most of us like to crown our efforts by creating a handsome label, or by buying a pre-gummed set at the local supply store. They would usually have a large selection of generic and not-so-generic labels and capsules on hand. See Section 9.

So there you have a rundown of the basic equipment needed to mess up your kitchen and enrich your life!

Your "Winery"

O.K., so you don't make your wine in a cellar! I made mine in a largish kitchen for years! So let's agree to call wherever you make your wine a winery....

My ideal winery would have a cement floor and a drain; a constant, cool temperature all year; ample workspace; high tabletops to store carboys and barrels and to facilitate siphoning; lots of headroom; a "work sink" with hot and cold running water; a hose and good water pressure; good lighting; cupboard space for tools, supplies, etc.; ample empty bottle storage; and, of course, a wine storage area.

Remember, though, if you are careful, you can make great wine in a kitchen, laundry room or spare bedroom! Everyone has to make compromises between their ideals and reality.

Your "Private Reserve:"
Determining Your Wine Needs

The best way of planning your long-term winemaking supplies and equipment needs is to figure out how much wine you consume in a given time period, say a year, and then work backwards. Once you know approximately how much you drink (and give away), you'll be able to figure out what size of production you should aim for, and accordingly, how much (and what kind) of equipment you'll need.

Maximizing a Typical Set-up

Instead of discussing all the pros and cons of various ways of working, let's look at one set-up, and I'll leave you to adapt it for your own uses.

A typical winemaker and her/his family might consume 2 bottles of homemade wine in an average week. The family would also like to give away, say, 25 bottles a year at Christmas. So, with lets say 50 wine-drinking weeks in a year, that's a total of 125 bottles of homewine!

Be not afraid! Using our five gallons = 25/26 bottles formula (one batch of concentrate or juice, or 3-4 lugs of grapes), this would mean we would need five carboys of wine a year (enough to fill one 25 gallon (110-115L) barrel, if you desire). Fresh juice is sold in five gallon (19 litre) pails every October, so the calculations are easy enough, if you want to go that route. Concentrates, when reconstituted, usually are in the five-gallon size, too.

If you prefer to make your wine from grapes, you've got to buy a minimum of 15 lugs to fill that 25 gallon barrel, with some left over for "topping up" the barrel during the year.

The Three Year Plan

Now, let's take it a step further and say that this home winemaker would prefer to eventually consume only wine that has been aged to perfection.

Let's also assume a minimum of three years of aging for the noble reds like Cabernet Sauvignon and Merlot.

Some winemakers can't conceive of waiting that long, but, please, let's remember that you aren't exactly twiddling your thumbs as the years go by – there's always another year's grapes/juice, etc. to vinify. The real tragedy occurs when you realize that your wine has greatly improved with time – and you have only one bottle left! Besides, there's a certain quiet satisfaction to be gained by watching the stockpiles grow – and knowing it can only improve!

This aging plan assumes that, instead of having two bottles of your wine to drink every week for the first few years, you'll have to drink only one, and age the other. This means you must buy one bottle of store-bought wine a week until your first batch is aged.

With 100 bottles at your disposal after gifts, this would give you one bottle a week for three years – but, the third year, you would be able to drink the 50 aged bottles from year one! In this way, by not touching any of year three's 100 bottles, by year six you would be able to drink two bottles a week of aged wine from year three! From then on, it's clear sailing: 10 years from now, you'll have been drinking nothing but aged wine for seven years!

I'd have to say that 25 gallons is about the limit you can make if you're a dedicated kitchen winemaker, but the number could easily be doubled to 50 if you have a well set-up basement or garage with running water and a floor drain.

Potassium Metabisulphite and
The Importance of Cleanliness
(Avoiding Oxidation and Air-borne bacteria: Two strategies)

Many home winemakers started with beer. Wine, unlike

beer, has natural acidity and alcohol that help to protect it from many evils – for a time. This can bail you out of a few honest errors but nothing can replace cleanliness in the workplace.

1. Cleanliness in the winery

A basic subject, but one that can't be stressed enough. An oft-quoted remark that winemakers love to repeat with a wink: "It takes a lot of water to make good wine." Of course, the real meaning of this is not that the winemaker will dilute the wine to make a larger quantity, but that copious amounts of water are needed to wash equipment and keep the workplace clean! From the moment the grapes, juice or concentrates arrive, everything that comes in contact with the wine must be scrupulously clean, free from wine residue, washed with a chlorine-based product like Diversol, and rinsed with a sulphite solution before use.

DON'T throw the remnants of tasting glasses back in the carboy or barrel. DO make sure you wash and rinse everything that comes in contact with wine with a sulphite solution, from wine thiefs, hydrometers and thermometers to stir sticks.

| *Cellar Hints:* | Keep your prepared sulphite solution (5-8 teaspoons or 25-40 grams of Potassium Metabisulphite dissolved in a gallon of water will keep six months easily) in a stoppered gallon jug, pre-mixed, for easy access. A quick sniff with your nose will tell you if the solution is still effective, for sulphite emits a sharp, acrid smell. |

Keep some extra sulphite solution in a "Windex"-type spray bottle. You will find a thousand handy uses for this gizmo: squirting bungs, stirrers, fermentation locks, carboy necks (give a short squirt to the inside of the carboy neck just before you insert the bung); barrels (to keep them from attracting fruit flies), etc.

If I'm worried about the surface of wine at the top of a barrel or carboy, I'll sometimes give it and the inside neck a precautionary squirt. The amount of sulphite absorbed by the wine is negligible. After affixing the fermentation lock, another spray of the bung and the lock ensures a clean seal, free of fruitfly-attracting wine residue. If you are scrupulously careful, and use these preventative techniques, you may find, with time, that you are able to get away with less sulphite in the wine.

2. Topping Up

No matter how clean you keep your "winery," YOU WILL SOMEDAY LOSE A BATCH IF YOU DON'T KEEP YOUR WINE TOPPED UP!

Whenever you take wine out of a carboy or barrel to sample, or when you rack, or (in the case of a barrel) when evaporation occurs, you must fill the container almost to (but not touching) the bung. A similar wine should be used for the "top-up:" last year's wine can be used for this purpose, but even if you have to go out and buy a bottle of wine – it's better than losing a whole carboy!

Cellar Hint:	When making wine, always keep any overflow in a smaller bottle, magnum or gallon jug (with fermentation lock) for topping up. Once you use a bit, you'll have to transfer the rest of this wine to a smaller bottle for the next time.

Cleaning Carboys, Containers, Vessels and Vats

The routine cleaning of carboys and the bigger vessels is made a lot easier if you have a hose, access to hot and cold water, and a floor drain. If you haven't, then don't go any larger than the 19L/five gallon carboy size. Carboys are not too large to be washed on a bottle washing device mounted on your kitchen faucet. After a thorough hot and cold water washing (a long bottle brush comes in handy if you are using a hose), a good rinse with a sulphite solution will be enough.

For equipment that has not been used for some time (like since the last vintage!), a deeper cleaning is needed. Dirt, wine residue and bacteria just love to hide in the little grooves and scratches that inevitably show up in equipment.

A good soak overnight with hot water and the chlorine-based "Diversol" (see package for dilution instructions) will get those plastic pails "whiter than white," and it will work equally well on glass. After the Diversol treatment, scrub down the vats with a nylon dish-scrubber, and a few hot and cold water rinses. Sterilize with a sulphite solution rinse, and use immediately.

| Cellar Hint: | After racking and washing, if you store your carboys corked with a few ounces of sulphite solution in them, they'll |
be ready to go the next time you need them: just swirl to cover the insides, empty the solution, rinse and use!

Cleaning and Conditioning Cement Vats

If you are lucky enough – and I'm sure this applies to a very small portion of the home winemaking market – to have the use of cement vats, these must be cleaned thoroughly before use.

I found two huge cement winemaking vats built into the walls of my basement shortly AFTER I had moved in, having been purpose-built by the Portuguese family who had previously lived in the building, bringing their winemaking traditions with them from the old country.

At first, I was repulsed at the thought of putting my precious, expensive grapes into cement, but, after a summer vacation in Beaujolais, where I saw many lined (epoxy) and unlined raw cement vats *les cuves de ciment brut*, I became convinced that I had stumbled onto a treasure.

I'll pass on the recipe for cleaning cement vats in the hope it helps even one person out there, someday. Thanks to the Thomas & Bertrand winemaker's supply store in Villié-Morgon for the advice.

Home Winemaking in France?

Incidentally, I thought I'd let you know that there are no

home winemakers, as we know them (kits, etc.), in France. Home winemakers there are people who own a few vines and make their own wine for the family.

However, there is another phenomenon which is fairly unique to France, which is "Home Bottling." Many rural (although I've seen them in Paris, too) folks will simply go to their favourite small grower, or their local grape growers' cooperative and buy wine in bulk, bringing their own carboys, *dame-jeannes* (demi-johns), cubetainers, etc., to fill up. There, the attendant will literally "fill 'er up" from one of many hoses coming through the wall, with nozzles like those found on gas pumps! The hoses have signs above them marked Cabernet, Chardonnay, Chenin Blanc, Gamay, or whatever, and feed from huge vats on the other side of the wall. (This is surely an enlightened country, wine-wise!)

Then, once home, they go to the local winemakers' supply store I spoke of above and buy a corker, a siphon, bottles, labels, corks and capsules.

Presto, they bottle and there's their year's supply of table wine!

A Recipe To Clean Cement Vats: 8-15 days before the crush.

The object here is to remove whitish tartaric acid deposits, grape grime and other nasties that have impregnated themselves in the cement's "pores," etc. We want to clean right down to the raw cement. Wearing heavy rubber gloves and long sleeves, dissolve 3-4 kilos (6-9 pounds) caustic soda in your slowly filling-up cuve (vat). This amount of caustic soda, which you may have to buy from a specialized chemical supplies plant, will clean a vat 4' X 4' X 6'. Fill up to the brim with water, let sit a day, rinse well (multiple rinsings) with cold water. At this point, it will be safe to get in the vat and, using a stiff floor brush, loosen the last bits of "melting" deposit on the sides of the vat. Rinse well, at least three times more, filling and emptying the entire vat. If you have no tap, spigot, or pump, use the water hose as a big siphon.

To save caustic soda, which is very expensive, you could use less by brushing or spraying a solution on, but to avoid caustic sprinkling, you'd practically have to wear a spacesuit!

REMEMBER: CAUSTIC SODA IS VERY CORROSIVE. ALWAYS CONDUCT YOURSELF WITH THE GREATEST PRUDENCE, ADDING THE SODA TO THE GENTLY-FILLING WATER.

To Condition Cement Vats

Once the vat has been taken down to the raw cement, it needs an even coating of tartaric acid to seal the cement. Coat the sides and bottom of the vat liberally using a new paintbrush with one kg (about 2 lbs) Tartaric acid dissolved in 10 litres (2-1/2 gallons) of water.

Let dry two days and use, after sulphiting lightly.

How To Overcome Your Fear of The Hydrometer!

Sure, you can make wine without a hydrometer. People have been doing it for thousands of years. Pick the grapes, crush them, let them ferment, drink the wine. Simple, eh? You can also cook without ever reading a recipe book, or learn to drive without taking a course... but if you'd like a tad more control than that, you'll need a hydrometer. Let's outline the various uses and basic operating procedures of the dreaded hydrometer.

Like many home winemakers, I like to think of winemaking as an art and not just a science, but I do use a hydrometer

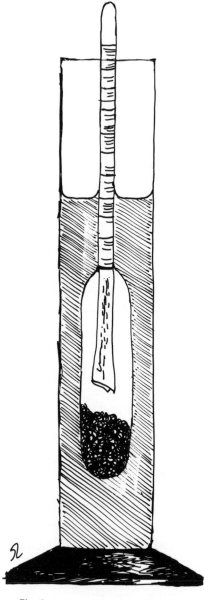

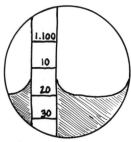

Fig 2b

Make sure to read the numbers at the lower level of the must, and not at the meniscus, where the wine clings a little higher to the glass.

Fig 2a

Taking a hydrometer reading.

– it's a pretty basic tool that lets you keep a close watch on your investment of time, money, sweat, tears and patience (Lord knows!).

Even if you've been making wine for 30 years without a hydrometer, why don't you come along for the ride? You just never know, you might want to make a change!

What Does a Hydrometer Do?

1 • it measures the original sugar content of your must
2 • it measures the potential alcohol content of your wine
3 • it monitors the progress of your fermentation
4 • it will tell you when a wine has been fermented to dryness
5 • it measures the amount (if any) of residual sugar left in the wine

What is a Hydrometer?

A hydrometer (or saachrometer) is a glass tube that looks slightly like a good ol' thermometer. It's weighted at one end, with a scale of numbers inside the glass. Very simply, this little instrument is called a "hydro"meter because it measures the density of water. Floated in a testing jar of pure water at 15°C (59°F), the hydrometer will sink to the point where it reads 1.000 at the level of the liquid. Thus, 1.000 is said to be the "specific gravity" of water. In a sugar solution, such as a grape must, which is more dense than water, the hydrometer will rise, floating higher in the testing jar, and indicate the sugar (total solids) contained in the must and give you a higher reading. (Fig. 2a, p. 28)

As fermentation proceeds, regular readings will show the hydrometer sinking lower and lower as the must becomes wine. When fermentation has run its course, if you take a reading the hydrometer will have sunk quite a bit, to less than 1.000, as alcohol is less dense than water.

Those are the basics. Let's put them into practice.

Determining Potential Alcohol

Procure a hydrometer (at about $7.50 to $10.00, you can't afford not to have one!) and testing jar. I've heard that some "Cadillac" hydrometers exist that have a thermometer built in as well, but I've never had the pleasure of meeting one. Using a sterilized "wine thief" or handy plastic (not metal) "turkey baster," withdraw a sample of the must and place it in the testing flask or jar, filling to the two-thirds mark so it will not overflow. If using fresh grapes, sieve the juice to remove the solids which may impair the reading, or better yet, let the must settle for several hours. If you do not follow either of these directions, your sample may read significantly higher. Before immersing the hydrometer, use a thermometer, preferably one that floats, to make sure the grape juice has come up to the hydrometer's preferred temperature of 15°C (59°F).

With fresh grapes, which are usually stored in cool conditions before you pick them up, you'll probably have to wait a while until your sample comes up to room temperature, but that's fine, your grapes will be macerating all the while (see Section 5). With concentrates there'll be a wait as well unless you dilute with water warm enough to bring the must's temperature to 15°C (59°F) – or thereabouts. There is a wait also with fresh juice which is always well refrigerated. Whatever your materials, remember that a small test sample will warm up a heck of a lot quicker than 19 litres (5 gallons).

Put the hydrometer in the jar, spinning it to dislodge any bubbles that may affect the reading. The hydrometer will bob up and down, and when it settles, take a reading through the glass of the jar at the surface level of the liquid, disregarding the meniscus, where surface tension makes the liquid cling a little higher on the hydrometer. (Fig. 2b, p. 28)

A typical reading for a table wine must (raw juice) would be about 1.090 (make sure your eye is at the level of the liquid to avoid incorrect readings). Now is the time to consult the potential alcohol scale, which is on the opposite side of the hydrometer. For example, at 1.090, the potential alcohol will read 12.7%, or just about as high as you'd want a table wine to be! However, you may subtract up to 1.5% alcoholic degrees from the reading if the juice has not settled, for minute grape skin solids in the must may be causing the reading to rise slightly.

Most hydrometers will have a third scale called "Brix" or Balling," which are, for our purposes, indicators of the percentage of sugar in the ripened grapes or must. A quick look at the third scale on the hydrometer will indicate that our example of 1.090 is equal to 22 Brix.

Once fermentation begins, we begin to note our further daily samples in a notebook, or wall chart, along with, in the case of red wines from grapes, the daily temperature. Regular readings will soon show the hydrometer falling – first very quickly, then more slowly as the yeast converts the sugar present in the grape juice to alcohol. Unlike past batches, where you've had to taste for dryness to know when fermentation has ended (or watch for the CO_2 bubbles to stop), the hydrometer will tell you exactly when the wine is "wine": the reading will be less than 1.000 (water density), usually around .998-.997. (Brix is fine for grape ripening, but once fermentation begins, we speak of the "falling specific gravity," and not usually of the Brix.)

The hydrometer is doubly useful for a stopped or "stuck" fermentation, for you will be able to see that, although the wine looks like it has finished fermenting, it is in fact stuck. You can determine this by tasting the wine (it will taste sweet) or, more accurately, by taking a hydrometer reading. A stuck fermentation is usually due to too chilly a room temperature, or too warm a fermentation, or too much sugar in the must, or the use of an improper (wild) yeast. In any case, you have to quickly get the fermentation going again!

To find out the Residual Sugar Content:

Another use of the Brix scale is for sweet wines that will retain some unfermented sugar. A hydrometer reading of the finished wine will indicate the total sugar content or residual sugar by weight. Simply read it right off the side at the appropriate time.

Learning to Siphon, or Rack

Siphons are essentially gravity-fed pumps. No more, no less. If you have never siphoned before, you may have many groundless fears about trying, based on memories of your parents getting a mouthful of gasoline while trying to siphon from one car to another when the fuel ran out. (Fig. 3a & 3b, p. 33)

Childhood memories aside, I must assure you that siphoning is an easy, essential and fun part of home winemaking. Essential because it's our only way (besides expensive pumps) of getting our wine from one container to another while leaving the sludge (lees) behind. It's all a part of helping the wine clear itself.

Here are a couple of simple rules to get you going:

1. To start the siphon, you must suck on one end of the

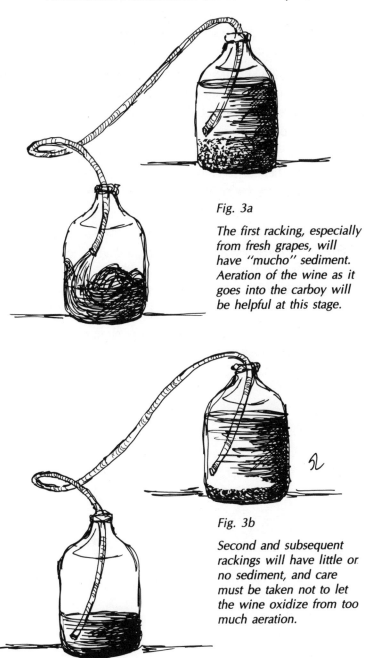

Fig. 3a

The first racking, especially from fresh grapes, will have "mucho" sediment. Aeration of the wine as it goes into the carboy will be helpful at this stage.

Fig. 3b

Second and subsequent rackings will have little or no sediment, and care must be taken not to let the wine oxidize from too much aeration.

hose, while the other is in the wine. (Don't be afraid, this is your wine, not gasoline!) When the wine passes the 2/3 mark in the siphon hose, quickly take it out of your mouth (unless you are thirsty) and point the siphon into the receiving vessel.

2. The receiving vessel must always be well below the vessel that you are siphoning from to take advantage of that "gravity feed."

3. The lower your END of the siphon is with respect to the SURFACE of the wine, the faster the wine will flow. If you lift the end of the siphon ABOVE the height of the liquid, the flow will stop.

4. If you are still afraid of sucking on the siphon, fill it with water, then put one end in the receiving vessel, and one end in the wine. The flow should start immediately, but there will be a tiny dilution of your wine.

5. ALWAYS rinse the siphon tube with water and sanitize with sulphite solution before AND after use. Otherwise, you risk introducing bacteria into everything you siphon!

That's all there is to it!

Section III

Wine from Concentrates and Concentrate/Juice Blends

Entry-level for almost everybody is making wine from concentrate, and it is an appealing choice for a number of reasons. Firstly, it is the cheapest and easiest way to make wine! Secondly, a batch of concentrate wine can be whipped up any time of the year, and, thirdly, only the bare-bones of equipment is necessary. Lastly, wine made from concentrate needs a minimum of time to be potable, so that you can be enjoying your vino in the shortest gestation period possible!

I know you're thinking "It can't be that easy...", and you're partially right. The downside of working with concentrates is that it can be hard to make that "Big Red" you've been hankering for... Whites are less problematic, but the heat applied in the concentrating process can sometimes leave your wine a deeper shade of yellow/gold than desired, although today's manufacturers have largely surmounted this problem. Nonetheless, it remains an inexpensive and edifying experience, and I believe you'll find your results eminently drinkable.

There are two ways to make wine from concentrate:

#1. By rote, following the instructions on the side of the box or tin. Not a bad approach, incidentally; you'll make consistently decent wine, but there's no room for adventure!

#2. By considering the reconstituted must as if it was fresh grape juice, and taking the required measurements with a hydrometer and making adjustments.

The advantage of approach #1 is that it is simple and repeatable, great for those who are into making wine to save money. Almost infallible, barring any major disaster due to measurement, or spoilage due to uncleanliness.

The advantage of approach #2 is that you become (eventually) a winemaker with control. For you, winemaking with concentrates is a starting point that may lead to making concentrates with adjuncts, from fresh juice, or even from grapes!

A Note On Regional Equivalencies:
What Kits Really Mean When They're Labelled "St. Émilion."

When you are buying the concentrate, I suggest you rely on the salesperson's advice. Typically, you will be buying a 1 gallon can or bag-in-a-box kit which will give you nearly five gallons (19L) of must when reconstituted. The store will most certainly have a selection of concentrates from perhaps 3-5 different manufacturers. If you're looking to make a burgundy wine from the Pinot Noir grape, you will be bemused to note that each manufacturer has concentrates to make "Burgundy", "Pommard", "Pinot Noir" and "Bourgogne-style" wine – most of which contain no Pinot Noir at all! To further confuse you, the concentrates will be from Spain, Italy, Australia, California and France, among others. Ask the salesperson which brands they have tried and have faith in, and have turned out closest to the styles they are said to approximate. See Section 12 on "Classic Wine Regions of the World and Their Grape Types" if you need help deciphering the plethora of kit choices.

At the same time (if need be), make sure you pick up a packet of the appropriate yeast, dextrose, and an "Additive Pack".

Getting Started Immediately/Let's Get Going: The Traditional Concentrate Kit

Concentrates are still the fastest way to get going. It's definitely the "as simple as making frozen orange juice" school of winemaking, but you'll have wine in bottle two months down the road (a few weeks if you like it raw!). It's a lot of fun, easy, and a good way to get a feel for the mechanics of winemaking.

Concentrate is simply fresh grape juice that has been boiled down under vacuum. In the vacuum boiling process, the boiling point is lower, and modern manufacturers are able to retain much more of the freshness and vitality of the fruit than in days past. What is lost, such as acidity, and tannin, can be replaced by the handy additive pack that comes with each kit. Some of today's kits have the acid blend, yeast nutrient and grape tannin already mixed in with the concentrate.

Wine Quality Rating: From concentrate, you will get clean, vinous, respectable wine, but it will ultimately remain simple, table wine. (And there's nothing wrong with that: half the world never drinks anything else!).

Let's Make Wine!

Before we start, the importance of cleanliness at every stage of the winemaking process cannot be overemphasized. Clean all your fixtures with a weak sulphite solution before every use.

Open the can of concentrate and empty it into the primary fermenter. To reconstitute the must you will need to add the amount of warm water and dextrose specified by the manufacturer. (If your first two cans of water are warm to rinse the can of the last bit of grapey goodness, and the last ones are cold water to bring the must's temperature to 15°C (59°F) or thereabouts (check using a floating thermometer), you can add the yeast fairly soon, after taking a temperature reading.

You should also add the"Additive Pack" (if applicable) which replaces essential acids, yeast nutrients and tannins lost during the concentration process.

Once the must has reached the "safe" temperature range for hydrometers, take a hydrometer reading to determine the specific gravity of your must. By knowing the density of the juice as compared to water, you will be able to figure out the potential alcohol and check on the fermentation's progress of your "Chateau La-feet." See Section 2 for the proper use of this indispensable instrument.

Next, "pitch the yeast"... this is a bit of winemaker's jargon which means to inoculate the must with yeast. To do this, you may sprinkle the yeast directly on the surface of the must. It is, however, always advisable to prepare a "yeast starter" beforehand to be absolutely sure to get a good jump on fermentation. Simply sprinkle the yeast into a small jar-full of your 15°-20°C (59°-70°F) must. The yeast will start to acclimatize itself to your must, and will be at full strength by the time you pour it into the main body of must a few hours later, at which time you should cover the fermenter with a plastic sheet and tie it down to avoid fruit flies and other nasties.

At this stage, it is critical to keep the must reasonably warm (especially in winter) so that fermentation will "take". Get that fermenter up off the draughty floor, and onto a table or chair, and half your work will be done!

After six or seven days the visibly-frothy first fermentation will have subsided, and you will be able to siphon (rack) the new wine into your 19 litre (five gallon) carboy, and fit it with a fermentation lock. This will let the new wine happily finish its fermentation in an "airless" environment. In the initial rush of fermentation, the wine is fine in an open fermenter, because it is protected by the volumes of CO_2 that are constantly rising as the wine froths and gurgles. But once the froth has subsided, the wine must be protected from the air by racking it into a carboy with an airlock. (Fig. 4, p. 40)

| *Cellar Hint:* | When making wine, always keep any overflow in a smaller bottle, magnum or gallon jug (with a small bung and fermen-tation lock) for topping up. Once you use a bit, you'll have to transfer the rest of this wine to a smaller bottle for the next time. |

After three weeks or so, when the wine develops a visible sediment on the bottom of the clear carboy, rack the wine into a clean carboy to get the wine off the 'lees' or sediment. If you don't have a second carboy, it's always a neat trick to rack the wine back into your primary fermenter, and then back again into your just-cleaned carboy! After 3 months, rack again, (fine or filter only if necessary), and bottle. There are 28 day wine kits on the market, but I would allow the wine to go through its natural process (instead of artificially stopping it), unless you really need the wine in a short time!

Make or buy yourself some fancy labels and capsules, and you'll have 25 bottles of your best to share with family and friends! In the process, you've spent about $100, or $4.00 a bottle, including start-up costs!!! Sit back and bask in the reflected glow of your efforts – and the knowledge that your next batch, now that your equipment has been accounted for, will only cost $50, or $2.00 a bottle!

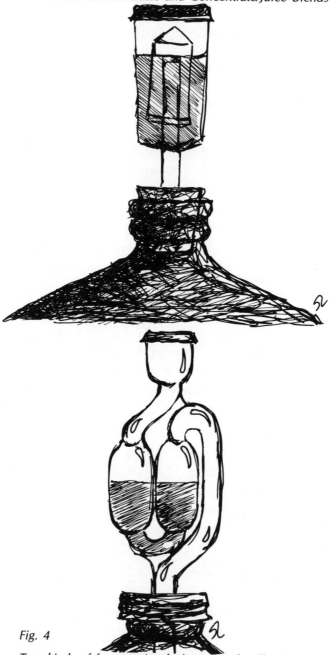

Fig. 4

Two kinds of fermentation locks, correctly affixed, one
with a rubber bung, the other with a screw top.

The 4 Week Wine Kit!

The 4 Week Wine Kit is definitely a symbol of the "I want it NOW!" times in which we live. But, it does have its useful place in the world. Positioned in the market for those who simply cannot wait to try the fruits of their labours, it also has the advantage of being useful to the more seasoned winemaker when a quick batch is needed (Christmas is a month away, or a friend springs a surprise wedding on you).

Basically the same as a traditional concentrate kit, the 4-Week kit differs in a few details. When the wine has finished fermenting, the wine is not racked, but fined immediately after fermentation to clear and stabilize the wine. (I prefer to rack the wine into carboys, but manufacturers keep the instructions easy for "first-timers.") The wine is then carefully racked immediately into bottles.

Because the 4 week kits are a little lighter in body and tannin than other concentrate kits, they mature quickly and attain their summit quite soon.

Wine Quality Rating: Consistent results, lighter-bodied wines made to be consumed young.

Concentrate Adjuncts

Making wine from concentrate is, as stated earlier, a bit like making orange juice from concentrate... to paraphrase "The Hitchhiker's Guide To The Galaxy", it makes wine that is quite like,... yet completely unlike the real thing. Orange juice from concentrate is good... but one always knows something is missing...the pulp? Should it be reconstituted with spring water?

In any case, we have the same dilemma with grape concentrates. Using spring water instead of tap water only solves part of the problem, and the spring water may contain trace elements that were never a part of the water contained in the original grape (but at least it contains no chlorine). Essentially, the water problem is a bit too esoteric for us plebeian home winemakers. What, then, can we do?

Dried Fruits

Here are a few suggestions. The adding of dried fruits to the must is perhaps the single greatest step one can take to restore some of the big fruitiness missing from most concentrate-derived wines. Dried elderberries are a personal favourite, for they impart colour and, (dare I say?) a bit of cassis-like fruit to the finished wine. Other options include raisins (I'd have to be desperate, personally) and dried grape pomace (available at your winemaking supply store).

The problem with adding any type of dried fruit to your must is that you are, in effect, simulating a real grape crush, and you have to confront many of the inherent problems of winemaking from fresh grapes. One of these is separating the spent fruit from the must (various straining procedures may be employed) and a second, more insidious is that, due to added matter in the sediment, the wine must be promptly racked, or hydrogen sulphide may develop. This condition imparts to your wine a most unfortunate smell... that of rotting eggs. Needless to say, the nose of your cherished vintage will be a touch impaired. An additional worry peculiar to the addition of grape pomace (and not raisins or elderberries) is that one does not know if the beginnings of hydrogen sulphide are already present in the pomace. Also, it is not stated on the package what variety of grape the pomace is. Cabernet or Concord? There's quite a difference! Still, you do get a richer wine this way, so it is worth the effort to experiment with adjuncts.

Oak Chips

An easy-to-use adjunct is oak chips. These can be bought in near-powder form for use during primary fermentation, or in the larger chip form which you drop into your carboy after the first racking. I prefer the latter, because, by experimenting with the amount employed, and the length of time left in the wine, you can obtain a lightly-oaked taste which will significantly improve the general taste of the wine. Over-oaking will result in a wine which needs extensive aging, and the fruit may even then have a hard time competing. Remember, though, that oak chips do not soften a wine the way the oxidative qualities of an oak barrel will, but the wine merely extracts oak flavour and tannin from the chips.

See Section 8 for a more in-depth look at the use of oak chips.

Concentrate/Juice Hybrid Kits

The "hybrids" as they are called, are an amazing idea! One day, some bright light was sitting around and had the brainwave to mix concentrate with pasteurized juice! Eureka!

Thus, you get a product, while being a little heavier to carry home than concentrate, weighs a lot less than fresh juice; a product that needs less water and sugar added to it and hence has a better vinous character; a product that has more body and flavour than most concentrates, yet is available all year round, unlike fresh juice.

It's a perfectly symbiotic match, and one of the best wine kits on the market! These hybrid kits vary in their preparation, so talk to the salesperson in your winemakers' shop before you attempt a kit.

Wine Quality Rating: The best are a lot better than the traditional concentrate kits.

On Aging Your Concentrate Wines

White or red, if you haven't fiddled with the "Four Week Wine Kit!" recipe to make a "bigger" wine, don't age it past six months. If you've followed a "traditional" vinification for a red concentrate kit, and have added adjuncts such as raisins or elderberries, your wine will need at least a year's smoothing for optimum drinkability! Lie your bottles in a cool place on their sides, to keep the corks wet and swollen... and their perfect seals intact. See Section 10 for more thoughts on cellaring your wine.

Section IV

Wine from Fresh Juice

Nothing is Easier than Juice:
but you have to be patient!

Juice has always been one of my first choices for beginners who are afraid of the mystique of winemaking, but want to get their "feet wet." Available fresh in the autumn from grape supply stores, juice is a no-muss, no-fuss way of making palatable wine that is difficult to tell (when properly aged) from the "real thing." Let the must (grape juice) warm up to room temperature, sprinkle the surface with the yeast, and away you go! Keep the wine away from air, be sterile, rack (siphon) when you should, and you'll have a real wine in a few months! Interesting in combination with oak chips.

Wine Quality Rating: Not bad. More body, more pure fruit flavour than traditional concentrates, especially the whites. The reds are light, but tasty. It's easy to be consistently good with fresh juice – if your source is good.

Today, we have the phenomenon of fresh juice shipped directly from the vineyard in California, or Slovenia, or Italy! (Don't forget to ask any local growers/vineyard if they offer a custom crush or juice service)!

The grapes are picked at the zenith of their ripeness, crushed, (with a touch of heat to extract colour) vacuum-sealed in a container, and shipped directly to your supply store under constant refrigeration.

Advantages: the home winemaker is offered a tremendous choice of grape varieties picked at their ripest, and a very palatable wine of some complexity and aging potential can be made with no more effort than a concentrate kit!

Disadvantages: The cost is significantly more expensive than concentrate; the juice is only available for 2-3 months during the autumn, and your entire year's consumption must be planned for at that time. (If an unscrupulous vendor should sell you one after that time, it may have "yeast-bite" from the natural yeast present fermenting slowly under cold conditions.) Nevertheless, you may find it a joy to be tied into the harvest! Last, but not least, fresh juice containers are unbelievably heavy! If you don't have access to a vehicle, you will soon realize why juice was concentrated in the first place! (I should know, having once walked four blocks with 50 pounds worth of Cabernet Sauvignon in one hand, and Chardonnay in the other.)

If you are desperate to make wine from whole juice, and it's the off-season, you can always purchase pasteurized juice. The choice, price, and *mode d'emploi* are essentially the same, except that the pasteurization process does rob the juice of a little of its fruity vitality. It does, however, make a decent product.

There is also an "Ultra-filtered" juice on the market that stays good for months, but then again, I don't buy that "Ultra-pasteurized" milk that doesn't need refrigeration, either! Proceed at your own risk, but do pose yourself the question as to the integrity of a product that has had practically all its fermentable matter removed!

Choosing The Grape Type

I recommend you read Section 12 very carefully before choosing your juice, for some juices are labeled by grape type (the correct way, in my opinion), while others are given vague names like "Entre-Deux-Mers" or "Châteauneuf-du-Pape." Look up the "Classic Wine Regions of the World and Their Grape Types" and "Grape Types for North American Winemakers" in Section 12.

Racking

The first racking of wines made from juice will be a little different from those made from concentrate because the lees will often be heavier. It is vital that the new wine is not left on the lees too long, or the off-odours of hydrogen sulphide may develop. This first racking also helps to clear the young wine.

You may be able to recuperate some extra wine from the spent lees by pouring them into a bottle with a fermentation lock on it. When the lees settle, rack this wine off into a smaller or half-bottle and save it for top-up. (Fig. 5, p. 48)

Aging Red Wine from Fresh Juice

Because you don't have the skins from which to extract further taste and colour constituents, a wine made from juice usual-

Fig. 5

Keeping the overflow (extra wine) in a variety of small bottles fitted with fermentation locks, ready for the moment they will be called upon to fill up the airspace in a recently-racked carboy or gallon.

ly produces a lighter, earlier maturing wine. Still, wines made from the nobler grape types will often take two to three years to reach their zenith.

Aging White Wine from Fresh Juice.

White wines made from juice may be a touch "green" in their first year, but, chilled, they're pleasingly acidic, yeasty and zesty! If you "complicate" your vinification by stirring up the yeast lees and adding oak-chips, you'll find the wine "fattens" pleasingly into its third year!

Section V

Wine from Red Grapes

Every year you promise yourself, this October I'll get into making wine from grapes. The season comes and goes, and your best intentions fall by the wayside.

There is really nothing like making wine from grapes – if you have any romance in your soul at all, you're bound to be caught up in the bacchanalia of the harvest! You may not be able to grow the grapes, but the beauty of working with them is that you have complete control of the wine from the moment the lugs land on your doorstep. Whatever happens from that moment on, be the results ethereal or just terrible, it will be because of your techniques and skill at vinifying.

Once you start making wine from grapes, autumn at your house will never be the same again – instead of rueing the passing of summer, you'll celebrate the arrival of the harvest!

General Theory

Whoa! Not so fast, you say! It may come as a surprise that many people start from grapes the first time out! It's not that strange when you consider that people had been making wine directly from grapes for thousands of years before science stepped in. If the quantities are small, you can skip a lot of the equipment purchases and have fun doing it by hand with friends! Let your equipment stock (crusher, press, oak barrel etc.) grow slowly with your interest and ability! Start small: buy three lugs (as little as 36$ for Grenache), and you will have enough juice to make five gallons. **Wine Quality Rating:** Higher highs and lower lows. You can make horrible wine from grapes, or you can make ambrosia! A lot depends on your attention to detail. Buy good grapes (spend a little more) and let it age a minimum of six months in the carboy/demijohn, and at least another year or two in bottle.

Where To Get Grapes

Most urban home winemakers, depending where they live in North America, will be using grapes trucked in from California. For decades now, North Americans of European descent have been showing up at the railway sidings at grape time.

The atmosphere is like a mini carnival: impromptu booths are set up as the grapes are pulled off the boxcars, and a midway sideshow of bartering begins.

Having myself been "burned" (my "Merlot" was not) at such a location, exciting as the whole scene is, I'd suggest strongly that a beginning winemaker go with reputable merchants where you may have to pay a few dollars a "lug" more.

California grapes are not the only choice, either: In Canada, Niagara grapes are available for those in the greater Toronto area, and B.C. winemakers can profit from the ever-more-highly-regarded grapes of Washington, as well as our fine grapes from the Okanagan Valley, and near Duncan on Vancouver Island. In the East, Nova Scotia wineries are also selling excess grapes, and one can expect the Québec growers to follow suit as new plantings come "on line".

In the United States, the dedicated grape searcher will find that there are wine growers in almost every state, and this has had some desirable spinoffs for home winemakers. Get in touch with the smaller boutique wineries in your (or an adjacent) state and find out who has extra grapes to sell.

If you're going to the trouble of making wine from fresh grapes, buy the very best you can afford!

Which Grapes to Buy?
(before reading this, see Grape Types of the World, Section 12.)

Each September, all devout home winemakers pay respect to the twin deities of grapes: The Holy Chardonnay and Almighty Cabernet. And each September, the pilgrimage gets a little more expensive.

Time was, a winemaker, once "bitten," could think about spending a little more on Cabernet Sauvignon and Chardonnay. The deal was this: pay approximately $10 dollars more per lug than most grape varieties, and you could be pretty sure of making a wine of some elegance, an age-worthy wine with a good mouthfeel.

These days, if you want to get that "Cabernet Quality", you've got to pay for it. Like any luxury, we got used to it, and, like any luxury, it has become very expensive.

Grape Expectations: Some Alternatives
Red Grapes from Cooler California Climates:

Pinot Noir and Merlot, whatever their provenance, are lovely alternatives to Cabernet, but, unfortunately, they're also just as expensive. Cool climate Zinfandel from Amador County in California is a wonderful option but, due to the popularity of "White" or "Blush" Zinfandel, it has merely become another member of the Holy Trinity! Some years, it is more expensive than Cabernet Sauvignon!

Hot Picks from the Central Valley:

Cabernet from the Central Valley makes good wine that definitely improves with time – and a little oak aging, if possible! It is expensive however, so the home winemaker should look at the other varieties available.

One of the best alternative reds from California's Central Valley (Lodi) would seem to be Barbera, especially if you are using oak barrels. Some enlightened home winemakers have made some ethereal wine by treating this underused workhorse of Italian origin to a little wood aging. Barbera has not yet reached the price level of the others, so it is still a good bet at the time of writing.

Hotter-climate Zinfandel doesn't have the pepperiness and acidic finish of a really good Zin, but it does make a lusty, if high alcohol, table wine.

Carnelian and Carignan both make nice Rhône-like, cherry-fruit wines that are good, if vinified at cool temperatures, for drinking young.

Ruby Cabernet offers some of the Cabernet nose, but it is an earlier-maturing wine.

Grenache, to my taste, usually offers too much alcohol for the flavour it delivers.

Petite Sirah – if you can find it – is a nice substitute for those liking peppery-dark Zinfandel-style wines. This grape, by the way, is not related to the Syrah or Petite Syrah of France or the Shiraz of Australia – but is in reality a little-known southern French blending grape called the Durif.

The other red varieties available from the Central Valley make wines which have less fruit and suppleness. They often have less potential for aging, and more potential alcohol!

Local Grapes and French-American Hybrids

While Cabernet and Merlot, and even Pinot Noir are being grown by every boutique winery on the continent, you're not going to have an easy time getting hold of these ultra-premium varieties. In Canada, and on the east coast of the U.S., it may be better to try for the French-American hybrids, which, despite all the razzing they're taking these days because they're not varietals, make solid, palatable wines. These vines are in increasing danger of being uprooted in favour of vinifera, and this may help your purchasing power.

Here are some names to look for: REDS: Chancellor, Baco Noir, Maréchal Foch, Chelois, and Chambourcin.

| *Cellar Hint:* | **FREE GRAPES!** |

If you live near a viticultural area, you may be able to procure some grapes for the cost of a little labour. I have some friends out west that get their grapes free, every year. They simply asked vineyard owners if they could make a pass through the vineyards after the mechanical harvesters (very important that you check this) had passed. For two years, they filled their pickup truck with a full load of premium Gewürztraminer grapes, and they spent a lovely weekend working in the sun, scavenging perfectly-sound, ripe grape bunches that had been missed by the mechanical harvester. They spent their nights under the stars, camping between the rows of grapes!

Tasting your Grapes

Pierre Chretien, one of Canada's most advanced home winemakers, told me several years ago I had better start tasting grapes I bought. I must admit I thought he was slightly, er, eccentric. But "no" he insisted, "You must taste all the grape types the store sells, or that you are interested in. You must take notes, as you would with a wine: this is the only way you will learn!" It may take you three years, but do it! I went away from that interview, thinking, here is a man who likes to do things like a traditional vigneron: he tastes the grapes, he eschews the use of cultured yeast; he uses a minimum of sulphite – he probably only racks on the full moon, too!

But, I started tasting the grapes that year, and I found out Pierre was right!

Tasting the Grape

Good winemakers, whether scientifically-trained or not, will always taste their grapes before harvesting. Careful measurement of sugar and acidity curves will tell you that the grape is ready to make wine, but only tasting will tell you that the grape is ready to make good wine. Witness this quote, from Larry Walker in *Wine and Spirit* magazine on Oregon Pinot Noir: "You can't tell whether grapes are ripe simply by analyzing their sugar and acidity... last year, ... the grapes were analytically ripe (high in sugar and low in acidity) long before they were organoleptically (to the senses) ripe. The only way to do this is by experience." And in the same story, from Terry Castel at Oregon's Bethel Heights winery: Two years ago, "... I could taste greenness in the grapes for the first time." Last year, "... I could tell differences in flavour of ripeness." As Pierre Chretien says, it takes a few years to learn – even for the pros!

If professional winemakers have one good reason for tasting the grape, then the home winemaker has at least two: to make sure that the grape she or he is buying is sound and ripe; and that the type of grape will be as stated on the box, to avoid getting ripped off.

One year, in searching for a good Barbera to bring a much-needed jolt of acidity to my California Lodi Cabernet blend, I noticed my supplier had Barbera from three different growers. The first to arrive was sweet, vaguely grapey, more like sugar water, while the second had more grape taste, and a high sugar content. The last to arrive was the grape for me, obviously grown in a cooler climate with a longer maturity time, with loads of grape character, slightly less sugar, and good acidity on the finish.

Out of interest, I tasted the Cabernet grapes directly after the Barbera, and it made the Barbera taste like candy, like a table grape: so rich, concentrated, tannic and complex were the Cabernets by comparison.

Learning Grape Tasting:

At harvest time, go to your grape dealer and take a few sound berries of a lesser, inexpensive wine grape variety. Crush them in your mouth. Notice the sugar level, rolling the juice around on your palate as you would a wine. Does the grape have good body? How is the acidity? Mouth-puckering? Merely tart and refreshing? – or even, non-existent? How grapey and concentrated is the fruit taste (not the sugar)? These are the constituents that will give your wine its character. Move up in quality now, trying to take notes (at least mentally) of how each grape tastes. Remember to vinify the grapes you buy separately, if possible, to prove your theories!

Learning From Previous Vintages

The grape harvest; September; the fever of fermentation – it all seems like ancient history now, doesn't it? Now is the time for cooler heads to prevail; the time to sit back and reflect upon what the past year has brought us in the way of winemaking – and what the approaching harvest will bring. Now is the time of reckoning.

During the crush, a mad craziness seems to envelop us – we make split-second decisions based on the gut feeling of the moment: Stalks and stems in or out of the must? A hot or cool fermentation? Sulfite the must and add yeast, or let nature take its course? Leave the wine on the grapeskins for 7 or 15 days? Add tartaric acid or not?

These are all decisions that can greatly affect the quality and character of our finished wine, and they must all be made in that precious two-week period!

But now, as the wine rests quietly in its carboys or barrel, we can take the time to make a few rational decisions for the future of the wine.

Firstly, taste the wine. Using a "wine thief" or "pipette," take a sample from each carboy or barrel. What is the colour like? How is it coming along? Has it been vinified in the style you wanted when you bought your grapes or must last autumn?

Equipment – and a Look at the Work Entailed

Too many home winemakers never seriously consider making wine from fresh grapes – seeing it as being costly, messy and expensive; and really not worth the extra trouble for the small quantities they produce for their own needs.

This section is written with the assumption that you are willing to do that extra work because you want the satisfaction of producing a richer, more complex wine. There is really no other justification for going to fresh grapes, price or labour-wise, unless you are planning on making industrial quantities of the stuff!

Extra Equipment Specific to Winemaking From Grapes

If you've made wine before from concentrates or fresh juice, you probably have a lot of the equipment you'll need to make wine from grapes: assorted carboys and gallon jars; corkers; siphons; hydrometer; thermometer you may already have will come in handy now.

But you will need other equipment specific to winemaking from grapes: access to a small crusher/destemmer to process the grapes. I say access because you don't have to BUY everything... if your friend is crushing grapes Saturday, borrow the equipment on Sunday. Alternatively, its always a lot of fun to tread on the grapes with your SANITIZED feet, or squish them with your hands, fishing out with your hands whatever percentage of stems you'd like kept out of the must. This only is feasible for smaller amounts of grapes. Remember, though, this is not just a lark for you and your friends: these babies are expensive, and these hand-methods employ quite a bit of elbow grease – you've got to work those grapes to get the juice out! (Fig. 6, p. 59)

In addition, you'll need access (borrow or buy) to a small press to reclaim juice from the spent skins (some people press the skins between two hinged boards and a nylon bag, catching the juice in a bucket), two or more (depending on your vinous appetite) good size food-grade plastic fermenters, and the requisite number of glass carboys, preferably with handles. Of course, an oak barrel for maturation would be lovely, but is not a necessity the first time around.

Grapes – The Extra Work

Now that you know about the equipment, let's look at how much extra work is entailed. The immediate advantage of making wine from grapes is that you only make wine once a year,

Fig. 6

*The passion of the crush: squeezing the grapes by hand,
or putting them through a crusher.*

after the harvest. (I never travel anywhere in October – the most crucial winemaking period of the year!) Besides tying you in to the Zen of the eternally changing seasons, this lets you make a large quantity of wine once a year, thus minimizing your labour outlay. You will find that the crush time, press time and the bottling and labelling time takes on the proportions of an annual event, and family and friends will rally 'round, providing cheap (i.e. free) labour and a thirsty atmosphere of bacchanalia!

The 10 Gallon (38 litre) Minimum

Let's examine the pros and cons of making a 10 gallon, 50 bottle batch. While this is double what most concentrate and fresh juice users would usually produce, it is really the minimum that I would consider feasible to justify the extra time spent.

Why a 10 gallon minimum? Well, one makes wine in October, and when you take the extra tannin (from the skins, pips and stalks), oak-aging and natural clarification into consideration, your "Private Reserve" should really only be bottled the following autumn. After you proudly present the lucky ones on your Christmas list with a bottle of your "Bordeaux-by-Numbers", you'll be aghast to find yourself with a mere 30-35 bottles left – for daily consumption and to lay down! This problem can be somewhat alleviated by making a second run from the same grapes (See "Second-Run Wine"), or by pushing the quantity to 25 gallons (roughly 100 litres), a number I consider about optimum for the home winery. Twenty-five gallons also opens up the possibility of oak aging.

But, back to our 10 gallon example. Ten gallons of must will net you 50 bottles of finished wine... and you'll need about 6-7 cases of grapes to make 10 gallons of wine, with some left over to "top-up." If you buy the best California Cabernet Sauvignon you can stomp on, that'll set you back about $150, or $25 a case, depending on the vintage, region and vagaries of price. My total cash outlay is $3 a bottle for Cabernet Sauvignon that's just as good – with three years age – as many of the $7-9 "Fighting Varietals." Encouraged? Great! Let's walk you through the procedure.

If you're already set up to make wine from concentrate, you'll need some extra equipment: a large food-grade plastic pail for primary fermentation, an extra carboy, access to a crusher to split and slightly squeeze the grapes, and a press to extract the extra juice. If you stomp or squeeze the grapes yourself you can save some money, but I wouldn't recommend this for more than 4 cases unless you have a lot of help! You also don't have to buy the press. Since the "free-run" juice always makes the best wine, you never really have to press the grapes! Just make a second run to extract the goodness out of them! A larger – diameter siphon is a good idea, as well!

A How-To Overview For Those With Fresh Grapes Waiting

Once the grapes are lightly crushed and poured into the primary fermenter, (I like to include about 25% of the stems for tannin – more will give you a greener, tannic, tough-tasting wine), you may pitch the yeast (or add the yeast starter), provided that the must is up to the temperature at which yeast thrives, around 20°C (68°F). Cover the pail (do not fill over 3/4 full) tightly with plastic sheeting.

Note: Before adding the yeast, you may want to stun the wild yeasts on the grapeskins by adding sulphite before you pitch the store-bought cultured yeast, but as this is a little more complicated, read about it in the next section: The Red Winemaking Process in Detail: A Word on Wild Yeasts.

With the onset of fermentation, the skins will form a "cap" (or châpeau) on the top of the wine, which must frequently be pushed back into the wine, or spoilage will occur.

I like to leave the new wine on the skins for as long as possible... seven to ten days (or more), depending on the condition of your grapes when you bought them. If you have good grapes, the longer you leave the skins on the wine, the more concentrated the wine will be in the mouth, and in the glass.

Once the primary fermentation has subsided, it is time to draw the free-run wine off the skins. If you have a spigot at the bottom of your pail, you will be able to draw some of the free-run wine off, but either way, you will have to use a smaller, sterilized plastic bucket to scoop the grape skin/juice slurry out of the primary fermenter and into the press.

Once into your carboys, the wine behaves like that made from concentrate or fresh juice, except that it throws a lot more sediment initially, and you must rack it more often to remove the yeast sediment and vegetable matter, or you may develop a hydrogen sulphide condition (that inextinguishable rotten egg smell).

Age the wine for a year on oak chips (or in barrel), rack as necessary to clear, top up the main carboys from your smaller "leftover" bottles every time you rack, and bottle when the wine is brilliantly clear and needs no filtration.

If you plan on using an oak barrel, don't transfer the wine from the carboys to the barrel until the first racking when it has thrown most of the sediment, for dirty barrels are the devil to clean!

While you're waiting for your wine to mature, you can be drinking your second-run wine and/or your "false wine."

━━━━━━━━━━━━━━━━━━━━

The Red Winemaking Process in Detail

Preparing the Primary Fermentation

Before the grapes come home, take a quick inventory of the situation. Is the equipment ready? Does anything need repairing or replacing? Have all the vats and siphon hoses been soaked overnight in Diversol and rinsed out? Prepare the workspace. Hose down the floor, or laneway, or wherever you're crushing the grapes. Get ready; as soon as the grapes arrive have your crew ready to go!

When the grapes come, give the vat and siphons a preparatory rinse of sulphite solution, and place the cleaned crusher or crusher/destemmer over the vat.

The Crush, Triage by Hand.

Firstly, never wash the grapes. Resist all urges to wash your grapes, even if you're the ubiquitous North American "neurotic-neat-freak" type. If even one drop of water clings to every second grape, you're in for a fair amount of dilution, not to speak of all the foreign elements you'll be introducing from your municipality's water system!

Next, stack the crates beside a table where your helpers can pull up one crate at a time, open it and perform a "tri" or "triage." Triage is the sorting through of grapes bunches before they enter the crusher. Stray leaves are pulled out, and unripe, mouldy, rotten or otherwise imperfect grapes are eliminated or set aside to keep them from lessening the quality of the "Grand Vin" – your "Reserve" wine.

It's a fun idea to mix all the substandard bunches together (regardless of grape type) and ferment them separately to make a rough and ready "Vineyard Worker's Cuvée" for refreshment at the post-crush meal the NEXT year.

The Yeast Starter

It is always advisable to prepare a "yeast starter" beforehand to be as sure as possible about getting a good start on fermentation. If you merely sprinkle the dried yeast straight from the packet on top of the whole vat of (often too cold) must, it may or may not "take." Better to allow the yeast to rehydrate and acclimatize itself to the new medium (your must) in a smaller, more controllable environment.

Sprinkle the yeast into a large jar of your must, which you have brought to 16°-20°C (62°-68°F). By the time you pour it into the main body of your must a few hours later, your must should have had time (artificially or not) to have warmed up to the desired temperature range (16°-20°C). Cover the vat/container with a sulphite solution + sterilized plastic sheet and tie it down. Within a day or two – thanks to your starter – you'll see some evidence of fermentation beginning.

A Word on Wild Yeasts

In Europe, where the wild yeasts intrinsic to the wine regions have been subject to the process of natural selection for thousands of years, it is possible, even desirable, to make a good wine by simply letting the wild yeasts ferment naturally. Yeasts are omnipresent in the air; they are also found on the grapes themselves, held in the whitish "bloom" or dusty film that covers fresh grapes.

North American home winemakers, however, are in a different situation. Our grapes come from more recently established wine regions that may or may not harbour the correct yeasts. That is to say, the wild yeasts on your grapes may not ferment out to dryness, but die off at 4-6% alcohol; they may produce volatile acidity, vinagery or bitter tastes; and they may produce hydrogen sulfide gas in the lees, which smells like a cross between rotten eggs and those stinkbombs you remember from grade school days.

That, in a nutshell, is why most home winemakers always inoculate the must with a good cultured yeast starter. The best cultured yeasts – and make sure to purchase the ones used for fresh grapes – will ferment sugar levels with as high as 15 per cent potential alcohol; will form compact lees; and will deliver a fresh, fruity tasting wine with no trace of hydrogen sulfide. As well, some of the "Lalvin" yeasts are "Killer" yeasts that nudge the wild yeasts out of the way.

To stun the wild yeasts before you add your yeast starter, add five Campden tablets per 19 litres (five gallons), or two grams (a good half teaspoon) of potassium metabisulphite (dissolved in a little warm water) per each 19 litres (five gallons). These doses are the minimum requirement, in keeping with the "less is better" school of today. Stir the dissolved sulphite into the must, leave a day or so, then add your selected yeast starter. You may reduce by half, or even eliminate the amount of sulphite used if you have a good yeast starter and the grapes look very healthy but, be aware, you are taking a chance.

At this point, you should test the sugar content of the must (see: How To Overcome Your Fear of Hydrometers, Section 2), as well as the acidity level.

IF You Insist On Using Wild Yeasts

One of the best home winemakers I have ever met makes California Cabernet Sauvignons that are not only indistinguishable from commercial products, but are so complex, elegant, massive and scented that many would confuse them with something along the lines of a ripe Fifth Growth Bordeaux, or a Mondavi Reserve in a good year. Of course, he ages them in new French oak barriques made and imported from France, but it is easy to see that his wine has the "right stuff" anyway.

Having known him for years and plumbed the depths of his wine knowledge, it always frustrates me that his wine is still always that bit richer and more complex than mine (the grass is always greener), yet we use the same grapes and the same techniques.

The difference, then, must come down to the fact that he eschews the use of cultured yeast; he has always tried to lead me down the path of natural yeast, but I have never followed, save for the couple of times I have bought a pail of white juice that was already spontaneously fermenting.

Wild yeast may have advantages in that it may take several different strains with different attributes and flavour characteristics to finish the job. These different yeasts – IF they are the right ones – contribute to making a wine that may be more complex than one fermented to dryness with one, cultured yeast strain.

For those whose curiosity is piqued, ferment a portion of next harvest's grapes without adding yeast (it may take a few days longer and some heating to get it going), mature it separately, and compare it with the wine made the "safe," cultured yeast way. All the way along, you're going to have to be even more cautious about cleanliness and sulphite. If the wine comes out well, follow the evolution in bottle, too, and take comparison notes on your taste tests.

Sometimes Even Good Winemakers Add Sugar

Sometimes the grapes, particularly if they're from various wine regions of Canada, or the Northern U.S., just won't have enough sugar to make enough alcohol to protect the wine. Many's the year that Burgundian vintners have to add a little sugar to bring the not-perfectly-ripened grapes up to a potential alcohol level of about 11.5 per cent. The French call this chaptalisation.

While the Californians might snicker at this form of "cheating," they're forgetting, in their smugness, that many a Burgundian vintner thinks the Californian idea of irrigation is not exactly kosher, either!

Each to his own, but the morale of our story is that the grapes must have enough sugar to make enough alcohol to protect the wine from nasties. A nine per cent dry red wine is probably not stable enough to age well.

So, we must chaptalize, or add sugar. Wine yeasts, unlike beer yeast, have no trouble converting ordinary white sugar to alcohol, so go right ahead and buy it (its the least expensive). If you wish, you could use grape sugar or fructose, but you probably won't notice much difference. Using your hydrometer (at the correct temperature), measure the sugar content of the must. If the potential alcohol is under 11 per cent (or 19 brix), you should seriously consider adding sugar to bring the must up to 11.5 to 12 per cent potential alcohol. This will take some math on your part, but you can make a calculation, based on a couple of one-litre samples, that will enable you to figure out how much sugar to add to the whole must. Add the sugar in thirds, stirring well and taking hydrometer readings as you go, until you reach your desired potential alcohol.

Testing For Acidity

The next step is to check the acidity, for alcohol is not the only element that gives a wine balance. Acidity also plays an important role, refreshing and enlivening wines. Too much acidity and the wine tastes "green" or "sharp." Too little acidity and the wine is "flabby," flat, and dull on the palate. A well-balanced wine is one in which the acidity sets off the fruit flavours, alcohol, body and extract in a pleasing way.

Northern grapes can sometimes have an excess of acidity, while the hotter parts of California can produce grapes that are low in acidity. For the purposes of this test, we'll consider the several types of acidity found in wine (mainly malic and tartaric) as one, tested together as total acidity.

Buy an inexpensive acid titrating kit from your "local," and follow the instructions that come with it. Although these vary, all kits basically function the same way.

The procedure to follow may sound mind-bendingly difficult for those who hate chemistry, but, in practice, it is rather easy if you read carefully... have faith!

The supplied syringe is filled with a measured amount of must (or wine). The must is then put in the test bottle, to which a quantity of colour indicator (phenolphthalein solution, supplied with kit) is added. The syringe is then washed, and filled with a solution of sodium hydroxide (also supplied with kit). The sodium hydroxide is then added to the wine, 1cc (as marked on the syringe) at a time, until it neutralizes the acid in the wine, at which time red wines turn black, and white wines turn pink. Each 1cc of sodium hydroxide used indicates 0.1% acid in the wine. That's it!

MINIMUM ACID LEVEL FOR RED WINES: 0.55%
IDEAL ACID LEVEL FOR RED WINES: 0.60%

MINIMUM ACID LEVEL FOR WHITE WINES: 0.65%
IDEAL ACID LEVEL FOR WHITE WINES: 0.70%

To Correct an Excess of Acidity:

If the acids are high, I would encourage the wine to go through malolactic (see Section 7), then cold stabilize the must (see Section 6). These two procedures will temper the acidity as much as possible by natural means, without adulterating your wine with concentrates or by adding carbonate, as some would advise.

To Correct a Deficiency of Acidity:

1 ounce (30 grams) acid blend added to five gallons (19 litres) of must raises the acid level by .13 per cent. Work your math from there.

| Cellar Hint: | If you live in a northern area, and have access to high-acid local grapes, and low-acid, shipped-in Central Valley grapes, why not blend the grapes together? This way, you can produce a palatable wine that may be greater than the sum of its parts!

Punching Down the Cap

Once must starts fermenting, a hard cap of skins will form, that has to be pushed or stirred back into the fermenting must. These skins are forced to the top of the vat by the release of CO_2, much the same way the release of CO_2 makes bread rise. Exposed grape skins are not protected by the alcohol of the madly fermenting wine, so they must be pushed under the surface of the wine (using a sterilized arm or paddle) at least twice daily. (Fig. 7, p. 71). A benefit of regular punching down of the cap is the extra extraction of colour, body, tannin, taste and aroma compounds that can be taken from the skins. Many experts will advise stirring or punching down the cap twice daily, but more rich colour and flavour can be had if one makes the effort to submerge the cap three to five times daily.

In the wine world, the wineries often practice *"remontage,"* which is the practice of drawing off the must from below and pumping it up over the edge of the vat and over the cap, wetting and submerging it in the process. This is an excellent way of maintaining an even temperature (fermenting wine is always hotter at the top than the bottom), but some small, "boutique" wineries still feel that the best extraction is to be had by physically submerging the cap at very regular intervals.

In Burgundy, some avant-garde vintners use a long, horizontal cylindrical drum instead of a vat to ferment their Pinot Noir. This drum has huge screws running the length of the cylinder, which slowly rotate to achieve a very even fermentation temperature with constant submersion of the cap. They get very big, fruity wines this high-tech way, and, for us low-tech home winemakers, it only underlines the importance of keeping the cap punched down as often as possible.

Keeping Your Cool!
How You Can Control Temperature at Home

One of the wonderful things about making wine from the grapes themselves is that the winemaker retains control over the style of wine to be made; with juices and concentrates, this is

Fig. 7

Punching down the must; stirring with a sterilized paddle.

more or less pre-determined by the producer.

If you wish to extract lots of colour and flavour from your grapes, however, you must keep the temperature steady so that the wine does not "ferment out" in a heated, passionate, three-day rush.

The technology to rapidly cool down (or heat up) musts has been available for some time to commercial winemakers. Usually it consists of coils wrapped around fermenting tanks, through which cold or hot water can be circulated. By using more sophisticated refrigeration systems, even the hottest wine regions of the world have been able to make classy, elegant, refreshing wines.

As well, there is the question of style. In California, some of the most daring of the "avant-garde" winemakers are fermenting their big reds quite cooly, at 12-16°C (55-60°F), while other equally daring, equally "avant-garde" winemakers in France are fermenting "hot" at 28°C (83°F), pushing up the temperature to an unbelievable 34°C (96°F) at the very end for maximum colour extraction, fruit and complexity.

Beneath these seemingly contradictory approaches lies a very real truth: there is a lot of scope for the home winemaker to experiment with temperature and grape varieties.

I like to try to ferment my reds at around 20°-25°C (68°-76°F) (although the temperature inevitably creeps up as the mass gets going) – yeast like operating at this temperature, and I find it gives big, fruity reds that combine tannin and weight with elegance. Cabernets made this way take three years or so to express their character, but, when they do, they possess startling finesse and elegance.

"Low-Tech" Temperature Control Creativity

This is your chance to get into controlling the temperature of your fermentation! Far from being tedious, it's an area where the winemaker's control CAN really affect the final product's outcome.

If the heating is on full blast in your area in October, your fermentation could ostensibly rush to a seething end in about three days, with less pronounced fruit flavours and colour extract than would have been possible with a little bit of care.

1. Ambient Autumn Temperatures

Considering the average North American climate in the month of October, the home winemaker should rarely have a problem maintaining a cool fermentation! Starting with a cellar, garage or room at approximately 15°-20°C (58°-68°F), one is already in a desirable temperature "window" to make a nice, hearty red wine. Open the door/window in the evening to bring the temperature down further.

Cellar Hint:	**ISOLATE A ROOM**

A specific room (or garage) in the house can be maintained at a desirable temperature by keeping the heat off, the door closed, and the window open a crack, but the other members of your household will find it more comfortable if your "chais" has a separate thermostat!

2. Solar Power

Put the heat on to bring the room/garage to about 24°C (74°F), and after crushing and adding the yeast starter, there will be a short lull or delay period until the yeast multiplies, and fermentation visibly begins. At the longest, this lull may take three to four days.

Once the fermentation gets going, back the heat off, and keep it off on warm, sunny days. Turn it on again at night (and close the window, unless it is unseasonably warm) as much as is needed to keep the temperature of the room from experiencing fluctuations in temperature. Yeasts like working at a steady temperature, and you risk a stuck fermentation if you let the temperature dip too low, or soar too high. Remember to keep the vat near, but not on top of the heat source. The temperature will be colder near the floor, and noticeably warmer two to three feet up (especially if you live in an old house as I do). Direct sunlight is a danger, for it increases the fermentation temperature too much during the day.

3. Coils and Hoses

Imaginative home winemakers have tried to emulate commercial cooling technology by placing coiled copper tubing or sterilized plastic hose in the must, and running cold water (periodically or constantly) through the coil, back out and down the drain. To me, it seems like an awful waste of water for the average home winemaker (especially when using hot water to heat up the must), and I'd hate the thought of the water running all day while I was away at work!

4. Ice Bags and Hot Water

A well-worn, but always useful trick to cool down an overheating must is to suspend a sterilized bag of ice in the middle of the must in the vat. This is easily done by suspending the bag from a pole or plank of wood that is laid across the top of the vat. By the same token, if the must needs to be heated up to get fermentation going, suspend a sterilized container of very hot water in the middle of the vat. Either way, after the desired result begins to occur around the heating or cooling agent, regular stirring of the must will spread the temperature change evenly throughout the fermenter. Alternatively, you could put a carboy or two in the "beer fridge" to cool down, then return it to the must an hour or so later. (Fig. 8, p. 75).

5. Frequent Punching Down of the Cap

A time-honoured and very inexpensive way of reducing the temperature is by "punching down" the cap regularly. Many home winemakers only punch the cap down because they want to avoid problems with bacteria, without realizing that the heat

Fig. 8

Suspend hot water or ice in a container to heat up/cool down must.

generated by fermentation is concentrated in the top of the must and "cap,'" and submersion of the cap in the must will help maintain a constant temperature.

Length of Maceration and Wine Style.

The style of wine you will make is in large part decided by the length of maceration before pressing. Depending also on the grape type, if you press the must before it ferments you'll get a light rosé; press it one day after fermentation starts and the result will be a dark rosé; four days of skin contact will give a medium-coloured red wine, while pressing after 7-10 days will, depending on the grape type, of course, give you a deep red/purple wine.

It's not only colour that changes with maceration time... the longer the wine stays on the skins, the more extract, body tannin and astringency the wine may have.

If you hanker for a really big red, see the entries on Pre- and Post-Fermentation Maceration in the Special Red Grape Techniques section.

Pressing the New Wine

Make sure you have at least two other people to help you – pressing is a fun, satisfying, but labour-intensive job. First, set up and clean the press: hot water and washing soda works well on metal and wood, but rinse well. Sulphite the basket but not the metal. If the press needs oiling, I like to use an olive oil – I don't want any "3 in 1" oil dripping in MY wine! Next, position a sulphited bucket under the spout of the press, with another one at the ready. Have all your carboys – and a couple of big funnels – cleaned, sulphited and ready to go. (Fig. 9, p. 77).

76

Fig. 9

*The press containing the new wine or grape skins/juice slurry;
squeezing every last bit of goodness out of those expensive
grapes. The spout at the bottom right yields the
new wine leaving grape skins behind.*

If you can draw off free run wine, do it, and pour it into the carboys, affixing a fermentation lock.

For the rest, using a small sulphited bucket, start scooping the new wine and skins out of the vat and into the basket of the press. Let the free-run juice run off before you press, as this will reduce the volume and let more grapes be accommodated in the press. Before actually pressing the must, push down in the basket with your hands to release whatever free run you can, then, with the increased room in the basket, you may add more crushed grapes. Most of the wine will run out immediately, and you will have to change the bucket under the spout often, handing it to a friend, who will then pour it through a funnel into the waiting carboy.

Once the basket is full, add the wooden pieces and press. Be patient, each time you tighten the press a few notches, wait for it to do its work. The most elegant wine comes from pressing slowly, and taking long pauses while waiting for the wine to trickle out.

Label ALL carboys IMMEDIATELY by grape type, and as "Free-Run" or "Press Wine." The decision over whether to blend these cuvées (press wine is reputedly richer and more tannic, but I have not always found this to be the case) can be made later, much later!

The Secondary Fermenter; 1st Racking;

When you are making red wine from grapes, because of all the grape solids floating around in the wine, the time for the first racking comes very quickly. Within a few days, the dense, hazy purple liquid in the carboy will start to look black at the top. As the black section (the clearer wine) becomes more evident, the hazy sludge is compacting itself on the bottom of the carboy. At this point (within the first two to three weeks of pressing), the wine MUST be taken off this huge sludge deposit or hydrogen sulfide and other off-flavours associated with spent yeast are bound to develop.

| *Cellar Hint:* | **RECLAIMED WINE!** |

When you are doing the first racking of (four or more) carboys of fresh grape wine into clean carboys, collect the "sludge" (yeast sediment and grape particles) from the racked carboys and put it into another carboy or bottle, topped up. After a couple of days, the sludge will settle further, and at least half the carboy will be clear wine. You'll be amazed at how much wine you can reclaim this way. Just make sure to get this "reclaimed" wine off the sediment quickly, before off odours develop. This time, throw out the sludge. Keep the reclaimed wine separate from the main lot until you are confident it is of the same quality. If not, bottle separately under a different name for earlier consumption.

Special Red Grape Techniques

Pre-Fermentation Maceration

With fresh grapes, which are usually stored in cool conditions before you pick them up, you'll usually have to wait a while till your sample comes up to room temperature, but that's fine, your grapes will be macerating all the while (see Section 5). This is called pre-fermentation maceration, and it's all the rage among certain small growers in Burgundy, who extend this period as much as possible, believing a lot of good components can be extracted from the grapes BEFORE the fermentation starts.

If you like the sound of this idea, only try it in the years when the grapes are perfect, with no hint of mould or rot, and even then, only try it on a portion of your production, and compare the bottled results later. Add the usual amount of sulphite to stop the wild yeasts from starting the job for a while.

Post-Fermentation Maceration

I would always read about certain châteaux fermenting their wines for 21+ days, and wonder how this was possible, when I could only stretch the fermentation to 11 days – despite my temperature-control efforts – before the cap or chapeau fell back into the wine.

At the first opportunity, when interviewing the *propriétaire* of a Bordeaux château, I asked how it was possible to stretch the fermentation time to 21 days. "Ah, well, post-fermentation maceration," came the reply.

Essentially, in good years, when the grapes are healthy and have a lot to give, after the vigorous phase of the alcoholic fermentation, when the chapeau that you have worked so hard to continually push down actually falls into the must of its own accord, just let it sit there and macerate.

As long as you can bear to leave it there, the alcohol in the new wine will be leaching goodness and extra body and colour from the not-yet-spent grape skins. As the wise old Italian peasant says to his impatient-to-press son in Angelo Pellegrini's great Lean Years, Happy Years: "We must allow the new wine to fatten on the opulent grape."

Just be sure, if you'd like to try this, that the grapes are healthy and the vat is well-covered. Remember, the big wineries can afford to blanket the top of their fermenting wine with CO_2. We can't, so we must be especially vigilant. Smell and stir regularly to keep the yeast working and the protective CO_2 rising. Spray the insides of the vat with a sulphite solution in your Windex bottle if it makes you feel better. You should be able to squeeze another week (after your 11-14 day fermentation) out of the grapes this way.

NOTE: 1. THIS PROCEDURE CAN MAKE OR BREAK AN ALREADY GOOD WINE. TRY IT ONLY WHEN YOU FEEL YOU ARE READY, AND THEN ONLY UNDER THE BEST CIR-CUMSTANCES.

2. SEPARATE THE WINE FROM THE SKINS AT THE FIRST HINT (SMELL) THAT THINGS ARE NOT AS FRESH AS THEY WERE.

Partial Whole-Berry Fermentation and Carbonic Maceration

Real carbonic maceration, as strictly practised in Beaujolais and other southern French wine regions to achieve a fruity, easy to drink, soft wine, is impractical for home winemakers. It involves putting the grapes into the vat, uncrushed (roughly 20 per cent of the grapes are crushed under the weight of the mass of grapes), blanketing the grapes with carbon dioxide and sealing the vat. In this airless environment, fermentation takes place in the uncrushed berries, while normal fermentation continues on for the berries that have been crushed under the weight of the load. This fermentation contributes, as a by-product, even more carbon dioxide, which contributes to the blanketing process.

If we can't have full carbonic maceration, we can mimic part of the process to get a fruity, early-drinking wine.

So, DON'T FORGET to leave a few berries uncrushed this year for fruitiness... a minimum of 20% whole berries mimics partial carbonique maceration, adding soft, approachable new-wine fruit to your wine. The 80% standard-crushed fruit (with about 25% stems left in) will assure the "grip" and tannin your wine needs for longevity. This process is especially good for getting the fruit flavours to predominate in hot-climate grapes that might otherwise seem baked and alcoholic.

Simply put the whole (healthy bunches only, healthy years only), uncrushed bunches of grapes, say, 25% of the grapes, in the bottom of the vat, before pouring the crushed berries in on top. Make sure not to include any stems with the crushed berries, for the 25% of whole berries will still have their stems affixed. Alternatively, if you abhor any stems in your must, you could carefully hand-strip the uncrushed berries from the stems, but this is a lot of work. Start the fermentation in the normal manner, and the whole berries at the bottom will eventually ferment and burst open.

"Second-Run" Wine for Those Without a Press!

So, you've made your first "Big Red" wine, having drawn off the free-run juice into carboys where it is quietly bubbling away. Well, don't throw out those grapes! Because you drew off the wine, and didn't press, there's lots of goodness left in those grapes!

Most home-winemaking texts would suggest, at this point, that you make a false wine, or "piquette". This consists of adding enough water and sugar back to the skins in the primary fermenter to make a lighter wine for immediate consumption. There is an abundance of yeast left in the skins, so that all you have to do is cover the pail and wait. While I agree with the thriftiness of this procedure, I'm less thrilled with the wine that results. Save it for the third run, if you must, for the grapes are still in good enough shape at this point to try a second run with grape juice!

Simply have 19 to 38 litres (5 to 10 gallons) of fresh grape juice at the ready, and pour in over the grapes. The must will begin to ferment immediately! All winemakers' supply stores keep their fresh juice under refrigeration, so be sure to buy it the day before you need it so that you can bring it up to 20° C (68°F).

Wine made this way is even better than wine made from fresh juice, for the tannins, colour concentration and flavours not present in the juice still lie in abundance in the unpressed skins! Make sure, however, to only try this in years when your grapes are in perfect condition; free from any mould or rot.

You can buy the same grape type as the wine you've already made, or pick something complementary (Merlot juice if you've made Cabernet Sauvignon wine) that will make a nice blend.

At this point, you should follow the procedures for making wine from fresh grapes, for that is what you have, in essence... a reconstituted grape crush!

After leaving the wine "on the skins" for as long as possible (smell the proceedings twice daily to make sure no "off odours" are developing), draw off the free-run wine from the spigot, or siphon into carboys, pressing the rest by hand. This wine may not need quite as much aging to be ready as a fresh-grapes wine, but it will need significantly more time than a straight-juice wine. If your juice source is good, it may even invite favourable comparison to your wine that was made from fresh grapes!

Grape/Juice Combinations: Cutting the Costs with Juice

Last year, just prior to winemaking season, I was ruminating upon the second-run wine technique delineated above, when the lightbulb went off! Of course! Why wait for the second run to add fresh grape juice to the skins? Why not make a wine that was fifty-fifty right from the beginning?

I reasoned that fresh grapes had advantages – you could

leave the skins on the wines for as long as you liked to obtain maximum colour, tannin and flavour concentration. The disadvantage – travelling half a continent to my door some two weeks after picking – was obvious.

With fresh juice, which also becomes available in the fall, the major disadvantages are that: 1. There are no skins – colour and flavour extraction are pre-determined, and, 2. Heat is usually applied in the crush to extract as much colour and flavour as possible before fermentation. However, the fact that the grapes are picked and processed at the peak of their ripeness is a great advantage!

When you consider that the price for five gallons (19 litres) of juice is about the same as the cost for grapes required to make five gallons of wine, the results of my thinking became clear... I had to experiment!

With a bit of research, I found a local grape distributor who was able to supply me with Cabernet Sauvignon grapes and grape juice from the same valley in California!

If you insist upon using, say, Cabernet, there is a way to cut your costs. Use this simple formula: 1/3 grapes to 2/3 fresh juice of the same variety. Based on a 25 gallon batch, this could save you $150-$200, depending on local prices, for a wine that will exhibit much of the same extract and elegance as if you had used 100% grapes. Using less than a third fresh grapes will lighten your wine considerably, while using more than half will not cut your costs enough to justify the effort. The final figures, however, will depend on the local grape vs. juice cost in your area.

If you have only worked with juices or concentrates up to this point, and wish to try this technique, remember that you are approximating a crush – and you must treat it as such.

A Word on Frozen Musts

Now that grapes are being shipped across the continent

from California in refrigerated trucks, as well as in the more traditional "reefer" train cars, we can expect to see a network rapidly established for the "next big thing" – frozen musts! I say musts, because some manufacturers freeze a higher content of skins in the juices, while others freeze basically the juice.

This is a new field that is quickly opening up, for it offers the possibility to stretch the "fresh" grape season over a longer time with no preservatives or additives! It is highly recommended that you look into this option in your area, particularly for those fragile whites that don't travel well!

It also opens up the better winemaking regions too: home winemakers used to Central Valley grapes may soon have the grapes of Napa, Sonoma and other quality regions within their grasp!

Section VI

White Wine Techniques

Although this section deals primarily with white wines from grapes, winemakers who choose juice as their raw material will find lots of handy tips throughout, and it is recommended they read the section through. Who knows? Maybe the thought of working with the grapes themselves will tickle your fancy!

General Theory:

Cool Fermentation and Avoiding Oxidation

In modern practice, it is no longer considered acceptable to ferment white wines with the skins (as is done with reds). Indeed, white wine contains little tannin compared with red wines, because it is made by fermenting the raw juice or must without the skins. Because of this, white wines don't require the higher fermentation temperatures reds need to extract colour and flavour. (However, see Pre-fermentation Maceration in the Special White Wine Techniques segment). Until recently, it was thought that whites are best fermented at the lower fermentation temperatures of 10°C to 15°C (50°F to 60°F) to conserve fruits, but the industry's leading lights are now saying that this is too cold, that wines fermented at this temperature all tend to resemble each other a little too much. They now advocate a fermentation temperature of 19°-20°C (65°F to 68°F), BUT NEVER HIGHER, which guards against oxidation and conserves freshness, fruitiness and aroma. I leave the choice to you – Have fun experimenting!

| *Cellar Hint:* | **THE FERMENTING FRIDGE** |

If you have an extra beer fridge, fiddle with the warmest end of the temperature control a bit and you may be able to ferment one or two 19 litre (five gallon) batches in the fridge, depending on the size of the interior. Alternatively, see Section 5: Keeping Your Cool: Fermentation Temperatures at Home.

Which Grapes to Buy? (Or Juice)

White Grapes from Warmer California Climates:

Unfortunately, most of the California grapes available to North American home winemakers are from the hotter regions of California (usually the Central Valley, or, at best, from the Lodi-Sacramento area on the fringe of the valley.) If you have access to white grapes from a cooler climate region such as Sonoma, Napa, Monterey, Mendocino, or Santa Barbara, count yourself lucky! Central Valley grapes tend to have had the flavours and elegance baked right out of them. Still, palatable wines can be made, and we offer a few suggestions here:

Chenin Blanc is a California varietal that provides good raw material to work with. When vinified in the big, buttery California Chardonnay style, it can make for quite a rich wine of some complexity, with decent acids on the finish.

Interesting things are also being done with wines made from

Sauvignon Blanc and wood. In California, the wines are fatter than the French versions and sometimes quite complex. If you can get either of these grapes in your locality at a decent price, I would urge you to do so, if not for the price, for the change. Sit back with a glass and a smile as you reflect upon the skyrocketing price of Chardonnay!

That said, if good Chardonnay juice or grapes is to be had, grab it! However, it will never be cheap. Another option could be French Colombard, which can yield a fairly lemony-fruity, if rather neutral wine.

All wines made from these warmer-region California varietals must be consumed within a year and a half of the vintage, otherwise they will become hollow on the mid-palate, and dull on the finish.

Local Grapes and French-American Hybrids

If you live near a wine-producing area, inquire with your local vineyards to see what they will sell home winemakers. Many of us prefer the wines made from these local grapes, for they are often fruitier, with firmer acidic backbone and finish than wines made from the white Central Valley California grapes that are trucked and sent by train across the country every September. In the northern parts of the U.S. and in Canada, winemakers sometimes blend local (high-acid, lower sugar) whites with California (high sugar, lower acid) grapes to make a more palatable wine.

Seyval Blanc, Vidal, Auxerrois, Bacchus, Chardonnay, Sauvignon Blanc, Gewürztraminer, Riesling, Ehrenfelser, Pinot Blanc are among the many vinifera, vinifera crossings and French-American hybrids available to home winemakers across the continent. A little research may be necessary. (See: Section 12, Grape Types For North American Winemakers).

Pressing the Grapes

Instead of crushing the grapes, fermenting on the skins, then pressing as with red wines, white grapes are crushed, and then the slippery little devils are gently pressed right away to yield their juice and conserve their freshness.

White grapes are slippery and hard to press because, unlike reds, their cell structures have not been broken down by fermentation, which releases more liquid. So be patient, be gentle; this is important because the purest, most elegant juice comes from pressing slowly, and taking long pauses while waiting for the press to do its work. Remember to let the free-run juice pour off before you press, as this will reduce the volume, and more grapes can be accommodated in the press. Before actually pressing the must, push down in the basket with your hands to release whatever free run you can, then, with the increased room in the basket, you may add more crushed grapes. Make sure to LEAVE THE STALKS IN, for they really help the juice drain out of the press.

Once you have completed a first pressing, you will be able to liberate even more juice by stirring up the pomace with your arms (add a little "elbow grease") and pressing again. This juice will be less fine, have lower acidity and greater tannins, so you may want to ferment it separately.

Don't worry if your juice seems to turn a bit brown after pressing: if you are careful and your equipment is clean, this will disappear during fermentation.

Cellar Hint:	**MAKING THE MOST OF THE PRESSED WHITE SKINS**

If you're really worried about the amount of juice left in the skins after pressing, you could always consider a second run by adding some freshly-bought juice, macerating for a few hours, and pressing again, or by making a "piquette" or "false" wine by adding sugar and water and fermenting a day or two on the skins before pressing.

Wild Yeasts and White Wine
(See also A Word on Wild Yeasts, Section 5)

Because white wines have a tendency to oxidize, they, more than reds, benefit from their pre-fermentation dose of sulphite, and need a higher dose. This addition of Potassium Metabisulphite will discourage the wild yeast from multiplying, and act as a powerful antioxidant (anti-browning) in the must. Once you have crushed the grapes, whether you are macerating them with the juice, or just drawing off the free-run juice, you should stun the wild yeasts before you add your yeast starter. Add 7.5 Campden tablets per five gallons (19L), or three grams of Potassium Metabisulphite (dissolved in a little warm water) per each five gallons, and stir into the must. Leave a day (this is the time to take your hydrometer readings – Section 2); add sugar, if need be (see: Sometimes Even Good Winemakers Add Sugar, Section 5) and acidity readings (Section 5), then add your selected yeast starter.

The Fermentation

White wines, whether they are from grapes or juice, always benefit from a rather more closed fermentation than reds. The simplest way to achieve this is to ferment in glass 19 litre (5 gallon) carboys, making sure not to fill beyond the 14-15L point (barely four gallons) to allow for the foaming of a vigorous fermentation, so that the wine will not overflow into the airlock. Once the must is up to temperature, add the yeast starter and go! While the yeast is multiplying it needs air, so DO NOT PUT AN AIRLOCK ON THE WINE AT THIS TIME; merely cover the top of the carboy with a clean cloth, or put a wad of sterile cotton in the top of the carboy's neck.

As soon as the most vigorous phase of the fermentation

has subsided you may bring the vintage together; assemble all the various carboys of still-fermenting wine into new, sterilized carboys, filling them to the top. At this point, affix an airlock and proceed with the racking and maturation as for any wine, unless you wish to age this wine on the fine lees. (See Fumé Blanc: Aging on the Fine Lees for Complexity). Remember, as with red wine, once the white wine has finished fermenting, air becomes its enemy, and the wine must always be protected by being keeping the airspace between wine and airlock to an absolute minimum.

| Cellar Hint: | **IMPROVISING A "BLOW TUBE"**

As the fermentation subsides, if you wish to protect the white wine from air by affixing an airlock, but you are still afraid that the fermenting wine may overflow, instead of an airlock, affix a flexible siphon tube to the bung, running the other end into a mason jar half-filled with sulphite solution, placed beside the carboy. Any overflow will find its way down the tube, into the solution. Change the solution when necessary.

Special White Wine Techniques

Cold Pre-Fermentation Maceration

If you want to make a "bigger" white wine, with more extract, and aromatic compounds, try macerating the grapeskins with the freshly-crushed must. Instead of pressing right after crushing, let the grapeskins soak in the juice for 12 to 24 hours at 10°-18°C (50°-65°F) before you press. During that time, the must will be leaching juice and extract from the grapeskins. Another benefit of pre-fermentation maceration is that the grapes yield more juice – and that means more wine!

Once you have pressed, a quick fining with bentonite, a clay fining agent, is in order before you ferment, to clear out the extra solids, tannins and other unfermentables introduced by the maceration (see Section 7: Fining or Filtration). Leave the must one day to settle out, and once the bentonite has deposited the solids (which it will do rapidly), rack the must and add the yeast starter. Don't worry about a little oxidative browning at this stage, this should disappear during fermentation. Remember to save the leftover "sludge" from fining in another gallon jar(s) – you may be able to recuperate some wine that will be handy for top-up purposes later.

Cold Pre-Fermentation Maceration
(with Pectic Enzyme)

When making country wines from fruit, pectic enzyme (available at any home winemaking store by names such as "Ultrazyme," "Rohepeck," "Rohament P," "Pectinase," "Pectinol" – all have slightly different attributes) is used to help break down the naturally-occurring pectin in these fruits which would otherwise cause a haze. In white winemaking from grapes, pectic enzyme is useful as an agent to help in breaking down the cellular structure of the grape, releasing extra juice and flavour compounds that will help yield a richer, softer wine with a rounder mouthfeel – and a bigger yield of juice, as well! Follow the instructions on the product as to dosage (usually, something like 1 ml. of pectic enzyme in a 10 per cent solution per litre of juice), and keep the must between 10°-18°C (50°-65°F), or roughly the same temperature as a white wine fermentation. These temperatures have proven to extract the greatest amount of good compounds without emphasizing the undesirable ones. Macerate from 12 hours to a maximum of 36 hours (but only if you have very cool conditions).

Some winemakers will fine the crushed grapes/must wine with gelatin, others give the wine a quick bentonite fining after the pressing, but before fermentation. (Some do both). This is highly recommended because of the extra compounds, tannins, etc., you have introduced into the must with this maceration. Once the solids have been deposited (overnight to a maximum of 24 hours), rack the juice into clean carboys, add the yeast starter and ferment.

Note: Some home winemakers claim that using pectic enzyme can cause the wine to age prematurely (I have not seen this conclusively proven), but if you like to consume your whites while they are young, say, by the second summer after the vintage, you should experience no problems.

Barrel Fermentation and Oak Aging:
There is a Difference

The distinction between barrel fermentation and barrel aging is an important one. Barrel fermentation is the actual fermenting of the pressed white must (or fresh juice) in the barrel, while barrel aging simply matures the already-fermented wine, and is discussed in some detail in Section 8.

The distinction is important because full-bodied whites (NEVER barrel-ferment a delicate, light and fruity white, it would be overwhelmed by the oak flavour) pick up a lot of extra complex butterscotchy/vanillin flavours if they are fermented in oak, rather than just aged in it (although maturation in oak is a lot better than nothing!)

If you are so lucky as to get your hands on a new oak barrel (although a previously-used-for-whites-barrel will be fine), and you have enough must to fill it, your taste buds are in for a treat!

Fill the barrel nearly to the top with freshly-pressed must, leave enough space so it won't overflow, add the yeast starter and let it ferment! NEVER use a barrel that has been previously used for reds or (shudder!) whiskey – white wines are too delicate for that kind of treatment!

| *Cellar Hint:* | **MAKING AN OLD BARREL NEW!** |

The time-honoured way to make an old barrel new is to have it taken apart and shaved by a cooper, exposing new wood (this can be done, usually, a maximum of three times before the barrel starts to get too thin to hold wine). Another option (but it's sort of cheating) is to put a handful of oak chips into your older barrel to give it some extra oomph, either in the fermentation, or the maturation phases.

Those who don't have barrels, or enough white juice to fill a barrel, can at least "barrel-ferment" using oak chips in the carboy. Not quite the same effect; the resulting wine is definitely not as complex but an improvement if you like the taste of wood and do not over-oak.

Chilling out the Crystals:
Cold Stabilization

You can get rid of those crystals that keep appearing in the bottom of your bottled white wine when you pull it out of the refrigerator to serve to friends. They're not deposit or sediment, but tiny tartaric acid crystals that have been precipitated out by the cold.

This is only a small cosmetic consideration, and not a defect, but you can get around it as a perceived problem the same way the commercial wineries do: by chilling the finished white wine before it is bottled.

Put the carboy of wine in the refrigerator, or a cold corner of your basement in winter, once the fermentation is completely finished and the wine clear, with little deposit on the bottom of the carboy. Keep it at 4° to 8°C (40°-46°F) for two weeks to a month, and you will notice that small white crystals (distinctly different-looking than regular lees) will have precipitated out on the bottom of the carboy. That's all there is to it!

But remember, it is difficult to be sure that you've chilled out all the crystals. Let's say that you keep the wine at, approximately, 8°C (46°F) for the month and the tartaric acid precipitates out. If the wine, then bottled starbright clear, were to be subjected to, 4°C (40°F) temperatures in the trunk of your car in winter for a day or so (or in some friend's too-cold refrigerator), still more crystals may precipitate out!

Aging on the Fine Lees for Complexity

Aging white wine on the fine lees has to be one of the few complexity-inducing winemaking treatments that doesn't cost a cent! When the first vigorous fermentation has subsided after the last racking, I like to leave the wine on the sediment for a month or three, if the lees are not too thick, to pick up some of the toasty-yeasty essences of the lees (sediment). If the lees are very heavy, which is quite rare with white wine, wait until the second racking, when the lees are compact, before you try this technique. Some winemakers go as far as to stir the lees up once in a while to heighten the effect and give even more complexity to the wine. (A similar technique is used with Muscadet, as in Muscadet "Sur Lie.")

Leaving the wine on the lees is a little different from red wine procedures, where the main worry is getting the new wine off the spent yeast solids, for fear of the wine picking up hydrogen sulphide-tinged "off" flavours.

Sauvignon Blanc + Oak = Fumé Blanc

Has the sexy lusciousness of Chardonnay jaded you or

fatigued your palate? Looking for a new winemaking challenge? Try making a batch of Fumé Blanc!

Fumé Blanc is, first of all, made from Sauvignon Blanc, one of the white grapes of Bordeaux and the Loire. In Bordeaux, the grape is often blended with Sémillon, which provides a moderating influence. The two grapes combined with the southern maritime climate, produce a zippy wine of good length with a slightly grassy/green apple character. In the more northerly Loire, the grape can be quite acidic, even steely, but this is counter-balanced by the big fruity mouthfeel and extra elegance, or "goût de terroir," that the grape takes on from the chalky soil of Pouilly-Fumé and Sancerre, among others. In fact the "Fumé" part of the Pouilly-Fumé appellation name comes from the chalky, flinty *terroir* characteristic the subsoil imparts to the wine.

In California, in the early nineteen-eighties, Robert Mondavi singlehandedly made the now-famous decision to rename his Sauvignon Blanc, "Fumé Blanc" and, with a little oak aging and marketing savvy, he started a fire that has not yet been put out.

His methods? The immediate transfer of the just-picked grapes to the crusher, cool fermentation and new oak cooperage were the tools that shaped the identity of his "different" wine.

California Fumés don't have the same *terroir* flintiness of Loire Sauvignons: here, the wine's extra "smoke" flavour is the spiciness derived from a short stay in new oak barrels. The barrels serve the double purpose of adding complexity and tempering the wine's herbal grassiness brought on by California's warmer climate – and some non-oaked examples of Sauvignon Blanc will attest to this.

Mode d'Emploi

To make a good Fumé Blanc, I suggest you buy a pail of

fresh Sauvignon Blanc grape juice – or the grapes, if you can get them – in early autumn from the most reputable dealer in your area.

I like to ferment my Fumé with a palmful of French oak chips in the primary fermenter, (not oak "dust," but 1/2" inch – 1.3 cm chips). As the juice comes up to temperature, it is important to have prepared a small jar of yeast starter, using your favourite yeast. The must will start fermenting rapidly whether you add your culture or not, and usually the winemaker will want her or his carefully-chosen yeast culture to predominate. On the first and second rackings, taste the wine before adding any more chips. Remember, we're not going for the vanilla/buttery thing that wood-matured Chardonnay has. We just want to add a bit of toasty complexity without rounding off the corners too much!

Fumé and Oak Barrels

I advocate the use of oak chips over barrels for this wine because of the quantity produced. Unless you're an absolute fanatic for the taste of Fumé, one or two carboys (that's 25-50 bottles) of the stuff should do you a year, so rather than a barrel, you are far better to keep it in the carboy and "cheat" with oak chips!

Let the wine clear naturally, fine (and filter if you must) about April, and bottle in May, and off you go on a summer of "smoky" bliss! Your friends will develop a predilection for your Fumé Blanc because it is such a great apéritif wine, but it will do equally well with seafood!

Willpower Wine

The wonderful news about Fumé is that it is ready to drink almost immediately, so you have something to drink while you exercise the necessary willpower to not drink your Chardonnay (and your reds) for a year or so. I can attest to the glorious fact that Fumé tastes great right out of the carboy in January, three short months after it was made!

Chardonnay and Aging

Chardonnay. The very word is magic these days. Chances are, if you're reading this for the first time, your eye was drawn here by the inescapable attraction of that word.

What's all the fuss about? To start with, Chardonnay has to be the easiest French wine word to pronounce. Even the nearly as well-known Cabernet Sauvignon is a mouthful of marbles by comparison. Chardonnay is trendy, recognizable, and tastes great. It can be drunk young or with a few years aging with equal pleasure.

Most home winemakers deal with Chardonnay as a fresh juice from California, although some use concentrates, and some the grapes themselves. Let's take a look at how much control the home winemaker has over Chardonnay.

The Naked Grape

What does plain, unadorned Chardonnay taste like? Chardonnay has no instantly recognizable bouquet such as, say, Gewürztraminer and Sauvignon Blanc have. What Chardonnay does have is a very full mouthfeel for a white wine, while still retaining a steely elegance and a firm backbone; a predilection for absorbing exotic flavours that reproduce themselves on the nose and in the mouth; it is grown with ease almost everywhere in the winemaking world; and, unlike most white wines, the best have a capability to age and mellow, gaining complexity with time. Chardonnay is a chameleon, changing taste in reaction to various winemaking techniques.

If you have fresh grapes at your disposal, consider macerating the grape skins on the juice for a few hours before pressing. Most white wine is made by pressing the grapes immediately, and letting the juice ferment alone to avoid oxidation. With Chardonnay, which has so much to give, prefermentation maceration of skins, to extract extra flavours, is all the rage and some commercial winemakers blanket the vat with a protective layer of carbon dioxide and leave the skins in the juice for as long as 24+ hours before pressing. This is more risky for home winemakers, but, if we have a cool autumn, and the temperatures are fairly low, try macerating the skins for 12 hours before pressing (See Special White Wine Techniques). The must should be kept from exposure to the air as much as possible to avoid oxidation. You could experiment with half your grapes to monitor the difference maceration makes.

Juices and Concentrates

Obviously, maceration on the skins is out of the question for those using juice and concentrates, but here is a little-known trick to try: stir up the lees of Chardonnay during aging, as do some commercial winemakers. This gives the wine a toasty complexity. (See "Aging on the Fine Lees for Complexity.")

The Flavour of Chardonnay:
A Little Bit of Aging

We frequently hear about the different "styles" of commercial Chardonnay, from the big and blowsy California style, the exotic Australian style, to the refined elegance of the white Burgundian "Aristocrats".

Which style is for you? Of course, much of the final taste of your Chardonnay is predetermined by the provenance of your grapes and juice, but you can affect the wine by barrel-fermenting it, barrel-aging it, or adding oak chips during the fermentation, and again later, during the aging in glass carboys.

One of the most effective techniques the home winemaker can employ is a very simple one: a little aging. Even a California Chardonnay tastes zippy and green in its youth, so set a decent stock of your Chardonnay away (minimum 12 bottles) every vintage for tasting two or so years hence (concentrate Chardonnays will not last this long), and you will be amazed by the difference. Regardless of the method of vinification, the wine will be demonstrably fuller, rounder, and more exotic in the fruit department, and, hopefully, you'll have notes of melons, pears, peaches and buttery vanilla poking through.

Naturally, these characteristics will be accentuated if you have used wood in the vinification, but, generally, you will find the wine tasting smoother and rounder with a couple of years' aging, with a longer finish than you remembered the year after the harvest.

NOTES:

1. If you age your Chardonnay for over a year without filtering it, you will probably notice some sediment has precipitated in the bottle. Stand up the bottle the morning you plan to have it for supper, decant, and use the cloudy heel of the bottle to cook your dinner!
2. It is always instructive to periodically make tasting notes on the progress of your wines, for "unwritten is often forgotten."

Section VII

General Wine Techniques

The Malolactic Fermentation: Helpful Bacteria!

Long after the winemaker's hydrometer and tastebuds say a wine is fully dry, the fermentation complete, the winemaker is often surprised to see tiny bubbles rising up through the wine in the carboy. If so, this may mean that the wine is undergoing malolactic fermentation. This very phenomenon has been happening naturally for thousands of years to old-world winemakers who would be shocked to find that their wine would start fermenting again in early spring, when the weather got warmer.

Malolactic fermentation is not an alcoholic fermentation, but a process by which a special bacteria converts the harder malic acid (found in apples) to the more easygoing lactic acid (found in milk), softening and mellowing the wine in the process. Although some bacteria are deadly for your wine, the leuconostoc bacteria that makes the "malolactic" happen can be very desirable if you have a very acidic wine (from Canadian grapes or those from the northeastern or northwestern American states) which needs softening.

But, by the same token, it can be detrimental to the wine's quality if your wine is already rather "flabby," or low in acidity.

Red Wines

In red wines, the malolactic reduces harsh acidity (usually a desirable happening) and lends stability, which encourages the smoothness that evolves with bottle aging. As well, red wine often displays more complex flavours after undergoing the malolactic.

White Wines

Naturally-acidic white wines, like the Chardonnays of Chablis and most other white Burgundies (depending, of course, on the vintage), benefit both from the softness (from the decreased acidity) and the complexity that the malolactic leaves in its wake.

Softer, bigger, low-acid wines, and here I am thinking primarily of California Chardonnays and the like, do not benefit as much from the malolactic. For this reason, many California winemakers inhibit (at least partially) the malolactic from occurring.

Encouraging the "Malo"

The preferred and time-honoured method of encouraging the malolactic fermentation is simply to raise the temperature of the new wine to about 20°C (68°F), (16°-17°C or 60°-65°F would be the minimum) immediately after the first fermentation and racking (for aeration and bacteria encouragement) has taken place, to encourage the malolactic bacteria, originally present on the grapeskins and in the "winery," to get to work. As well, by leaving the wine on the lees as long as possible before each racking, you are giving the bacteria a favourable environment in which to multiply. If you are using an oak barrel, there will be enough leuconostoc bacteria left in the wood to start the malolactic off like clockwork every year.

The malolactic fermentation may be induced by a special culture of the leuconostoc bacteria (devilishly hard to find in some areas) that is introduced into the wine after the first fermentation is complete. Once the malolactic has begun, DO NOT bottle the wine until the bubbles have completely stopped, unless you would like to trap CO_2 bubbles in the wine. Woe to the winemaker who bottles before the spring malolactic! It's a good idea, then, never to bottle any wine until it's at least six months old.

Note: If you have made wine from low-acid CALIFORNIA GRAPES, and are still encouraging a malolactic fermentation (for reasons of complexity in your wine), or are observing a spontaneous one, be aware that the other, more harmful species of lactic acid thrives on a low-acid medium such as California wine. To avoid any problems:

1. KEEP ALL CONTAINERS FULLY TOPPED UP.
2. SULPHITE AT THE RATE OF ONE GRAM PER 5 LITRES (ONE GRAM PER GALLON) AT THE TIME OF THE FIRST RACKING AFTER THE MALOLACTIC IS COMPLETE TO AVOID OTHER UNDESIRABLE BACTERIA.
3. KEEP THE MATURING WINE AS COOL AS POSSIBLE.

Avoiding the Malolactic Fermentation

To discourage the malolactic (especially in low-acid California wines), keep the temperature of your cellar below 15°C (58°F), and rack the wine off its lees whenever they appear. One can also keep the sulphite level fairly high, but monitoring total sulphite levels is beyond the scope of the average home winemaker. One gram of SO_2 per 19 litres (five gallons) of must, added at each racking, will be a safe level that we can live with without constantly measuring. As well, if you take this route, you will be protecting your wine against other, harmful lactic bacteria.

Partial Malo!

Partial malolactic fermentation is a bit of a misnomer. It does not refer to the bottling or arresting of a wine when it is still undergoing malolactic, but rather, to the blending of specific lots of wine that have undergone complete malolactic fermentation with others that have not. In the commercial world, wily hot-climate winemakers use this technique in their struggle to strike the best compromise between elegance, complexity, and firm acidic backbone.

Home winemakers who hope to try this technique should remember that this is "A-Level" stuff here. There is no guarantee that you can prevent the malo in one lot while encouraging it in the other. Even if you succeed, I can give you no assurance that the combined wines will taste better than the sum of their parts! Still, a challenge has never stopped us before, has it?!

Cellar Hint: **TRAPPING THE MALOLACTIC**

While I have spoken about preventing the malolactic from occurring, and encouraging it to complete its course, it should be mentioned that several wine styles make a virtue of trapping the malolactic in mid-flight. These wines are all slightly fizzy, for the carbon dioxide that is given off by the malolactic becomes dissolved into the wine. When the malolactic occurs in carboy, it can bubble out of the airlock, but in the bottle it cannot get past the cork.

Red fizzy Lambrusco for Emilia-Romagna in Italy, scores of slightly "frizzante" white wines from northern Italy, the Portuguese white Vinho Verde and the rosés (Mateus, Faïsca etc.), as well, are all famous examples of wines that have a slight "prickle" on the tongue – a sure sign of what I call the "trapped malolactic."

If you want to emulate one of these styles, simply wait for the malolactic to occur (or induce it), let it go on for a few days, then bottle while the wine is still bubbling.

Further Rackings and Clarification

Is the wine brilliantly clear in the carboy? Perhaps the best method of clearing a wine is allowing Father Time to do it for you. Given enough time, if you are patient and willing to let your wine stay in the carboy/barrel for nearly a year, it should "fall" completely clear of its own accord, without any help from you. A good test is to shine a flashlight through the carboy: if you can see the beam in the liquid, it isn't clear enough yet, and would, eventually make a considerable deposit in the bottle.

If the wine is nearly clear enough, and you're past the six month mark, my gut feeling is: don't fine! With a schedule alternating between careful (watch the oxidation) racking and waiting, the wine will fall clear of its own accord.

Fining or Filtration?

The decision of whether to fine or not is really just a question of time. If the wine has a persistent cloudy haze come spring, or if you want to bottle the wine early, for whatever reason, you may have to resort to fining, or even filtration. Be careful, though, for one can "overfilter" and remove flavour and complexity along with those microscopic solids!

In my opinion, wines that need that "extra polish," as whites often do, should be fined, but never filtered. To please consumers, some wines are filtered to the point that they are eviscerated and don't have enough life left in them to age in bottle, let alone the energy to throw a deposit.

While the filtration is removing the microscopic solids that cause a wine to be cloudy, it can also remove flavour, colour and bouquet. Filtration may be acceptable for commercial mass producers who want repeatable, mass market, "starbright" products that will not offend customers, but remember that their filtration equipment is a lot more sophisticated than anything you can readily get your hands on. The home winemaker is much more likely to oxidize his or her wine while trying to clear it. This is my personal opinion, and not one that every winemaking book agrees with. If you want to filter, get a second opinion from your local home winemaking store. They will often rent filtration systems on the premises. Whatever system you choose, always start with the coarsest filter, which will remove only the biggest solids, and work up to finer-pored filters if the problem persists. Do be aware, however, that many find their wines taste flatter, but look cosmetically better, after filtration. There's a moral in there somewhere.

Fining

When the combination of regular racking and time fails to clear a wine, fining can be considered as a more acceptable, organic alternative to filtration. It is easier to accomplish, and it robs much less of the wine's vitality. There are many different substances that one can use to fine a wine, and while old favourites like ox blood have been used in Burgundy for centuries, I have included only those appropriate for the basement chais, unless of course, you know a butcher who specializes in freshly-killed oxen!

The various fining agents basically all work the same way: mixed in with the wine, they form an electrical bond with the suspended particles that are causing the cloudiness (opposites attract – similar charges repel). As the fining agent settles to the bottom of the carboy, it pulls the suspended particles with it, clearing the wine. After a period of four days to three weeks or so, when the wine has cleared, it is racked off these lees, and bottled.

Fining Agents and Their Uses

Remember: opposites attract! Most hazes can be dealt with by matching up the electrical charge of the suspended matter with that of the fining agent. Protein hazes (often found in white wine) are positively-charged, so bentonite, a negatively-charged agent, will combine with (and drag down) the suspended matter in most white wines. Putting a positively-charged fining agent in a white wine often clouds the wine further, as all these little positive particles – suspending matter and fining agent – float around repelling each other (like guests at a bad cocktail party)! In red wine, where the suspended matter is usually negatively-charged tannin and colouring matter-based (polyphenols), egg whites and gelatin do a better job.

The fining agents below are preceded by their electrical charge.

«+» Egg Whites, or Albumen, is the most time-honoured (and perhaps best), fining method available to the home winemaker. The tannins and colour in red wine are significantly reduced by fining with egg whites, so only reds with lots of tannic aging potential should be considered. One simply gently beats the egg white into a froth (but not a stiff froth, which cannot be easily stirred in) before mixing with the wine. One half egg white will suffice for 19 litres (5 gallons) of wine.

«+» Gelatine is a very powerful fining agent that must be used carefully to avoid overfining. It, too, removes tannin and colouring matter as well as clearing the wine. Read the instructions on the package before using, but never boil gelatin solutions! Some winemakers even add tannin before fining, so that there will be no loss.

«+» Isinglass is a fining agent made from the bladder of sturgeon. It must be made into solution in much the same manner as gelatine, and has the advantage of being the most gentle of the organic finings.

«+» Sparkalloid is made from seaweed, and must be boiled into solution to be effective, so see the package for details. Because it leaves a compact, firm sediment, Sparkalloid is sometimes used as a polishing fining to make a previous fining agent's sediment more compact.

«–» Bentonite, a pure clay from Wyoming, removes the least colour and tannin from a wine, but tends to deposit a larger, fluffier lees than the other methods, which can result in a loss of wine at racking time. At that time, pour the lees into a smaller bottle, fit it with a fermentation lock, and you will be able to recuperate a little more of the wine as it settles further. Bentonite is particularly valuable, as it carries a negative charge, and can be used to clear a haze that has been worsened by the addition of a positively-charged fining agent.

Bentonite usually comes as a fine grey powder that must be boiled and whisked into a slurry before stirring into the wine.

Oak Chips are only "fair" as a clearing agent, but make the only such agent that actually adds a desirable taste (and some tannin) to the wine as they sink. In addition, oak chips "rob" precious little of the wine's intrinsic character.

The Art of Blending:
the Concept of the "Reserve" Wine

In the autumn, when you are deliberating over which grapes/juices to buy, consider new and daring "assemblages" to cut costs and sharpen your winemaking (and tasting) skills, improving your wine along the way!

Some people believe that, after tasting the grapes (see: Tasting Your Grapes, Section 5), the grapes should be blended in the primary fermentation vessel. Advocates of this approach say that a richer, more seamless wine results from this technique. The obvious drawback is that you must make your blending decisions right at the beginning, based on your impressions from tasting the grapes.

The more common solution is to make two batches of wine. For those looking at cutting down costs, this may be the route to go. Using red California grapes as an example, you could make one large lot of one of the following inexpensive, but decent varieties: Barbera, Carignan, Ruby Cabernet, or Carnelian. Make a second lot that is 100 per cent of a more "noble" variety. (These can cost up to twice as much as the inexpensive varieties – Cabernet Sauvignon, Cabernet Franc, Merlot or Pinot Noir or cool-climate Zinfandel.)

When the wine is 3-6 months old, conduct careful taste tests (make an event of it – friends will love it!) in which you blend varying amounts of the "noble" wine with your inexpensive wine. From this, you should be able to come up with the percentages that will make your "Reserve" wine.

Next, blend the wines by the predetermined percentages in the carboy/barrel, and allow at least a month or two for them to marry, then allow some further time for a little bottle age.

In the meantime, bottle and use the rest of your inexpensive varietal as your "everyday" wine while you wait for your "Reserve" to mature.

Alternatively, if you find the quality of the more expensive wine is totally compromised when any proportion of the inexpensive wine is added, you may elect to bottle them separately.

Section VIII

Wine Maturation

Oaking – Chips or Barrels?

Making the Decision

The home winemaker will face many pivotal choices in the course of her or his winemaking, but perhaps none carries the weight of responsibility as does the decision to begin barrel-aging wine.

Behind every achievement in life there lurks a plateau: but, let's face it, plateaus are not all bad, especially if you're already a success at what you're doing. The analogy holds for the home winemaker: if you're getting a good result without oak barrels, you might be reticent to change.

Are Chips For You?

Oak chips are a blessing to the home winemaker: they are inexpensive, and require no maintenance, as oak barrels do.

What's more, they add a pleasant oaky-vanilla taste to your wine, if used properly.

Oak chips can be bought in near-powder form for use during primary fermentation, or in the larger chip form (approx 1/2" long) (1.3 cm) which you drop into your carboy during fermentation, and/or after the first racking. I prefer the latter, because, by experimenting with the amount employed, and the length of time the chips macerate in the wine, you can obtain a lightly-oaked taste which will significantly improve the general taste of the wine. Over-oaking will result in a wine which needs extensive aging, and even then the fruit may have a hard time competing and the wine will have a dry, harsh, woody finish. Remember, though, that oak chips do not soften a wine the way the oxidative qualities of an oak barrel will; the wine merely extracts oak flavour and tannin from the chips.

For purists who resist fining their wine, oak chips have the additional benefit of acting as clarifiers. As they slowly settle to the bottom of the carboy, they attract colloidal particles, clearing the wine, and adding flavour and tannins en route.

Mode d'emploi

While many books offer you a recipe for the amount of oak chips to use for a 19 litre (five gallon) batch of wine, I have found over time that a winemaker's tastebuds are the best yardstick to go by.

When racking, one simply puts a scant palmful of sulphited (sterilised) French or American white oak chips into the bottom of the carboy: these will rise as it fills, to later slowly sink to the bottom. Each subsequent time you rack the wine, taste it to determine the effect the chips have had on your wine's flavour. An inexpensive gadget called a "pipette" or "wine thief" is perfect for this purpose, and more glamorous than your siphon-hose!

Add a fresh palmful of chips to the new carboy, and discard the previous chips, which have done their best to "oak" and clarify. Any wine you plan to age a year or more in bottle can be oaked slightly more than "just so," as the woody taste will mellow with time. Be careful with the quantity of chips you use, and keep the style of wine you want firmly in mind each time you taste for the oak flavour. Remember that sometimes "the ultimate art of the winemaker is to know when to do nothing," as Hugh Johnson once wrote.

The Oak Barrel

Why should you get into oak barrels if the chips are so darn good? Ay, there's the rub... Can the average person tell the difference between a wine aged on chips and one aged in a barrel? Oh, God, Yes! Unquestionably yes! Emphatically YES!

And that's where the "pivotal choice" comes in – Barrels are a pain in the punt, but mature barrel-aged wine can be like the nectar of the gods! I've tasted chip-oaked and judiciously barrel-oaked cuvées side-by-side ... Chips vs. Barrel: Same grapes, same year, and I promise you that even a teetotaller could tell the glorious difference!

As the months pass, the barrel absorbs minute quantities of oxygen into the wine, and, at the same time, a minimal portion of the wine evaporates through the staves of the barrel. This serendipitous give-and-take relationship is what gives the wine a roundness, mellowness and complexity it could never attain in an inert container like glass. Aging in barrique helps the wine precipitate (throw) its tartar crystals, its excess colouring matter, tannin and astringency. As well, barrel aging helps a wine develop the complexity of its bouquet through the controlled oxidation that occurs over the months the wine is maturing. The oak cask is truly yet another marvel of nature!

The Stress of Owning a Barrel

Life would be a lot easier if the only criteria for getting into oak barrels were price. Barrel maintenance and commitment are the issues here! Barrels must always be kept full or they become much more prone to airborne bacteria and vinegar yeasts. Also, an empty barrel risks shrinkage of its staves (and leakage). This of course brings modern man right back to the ancient rite of leaving the wine in barrel all year, from one harvest until the next. Once bottled, the new wine takes its rightful place where the old had been.

That said, I must confuse matters by saying that there is no agreement among winemakers as to how long a wine should stay in barrel, however, the smaller the barrel, the more wine will come in contact with the oak. New barrels impart more oak flavour to the wine; hence, every year the barrel is used, the effect is more subtle, and the wine can spend a longer time in contact with the wood. Old barrels can be taken apart and shaved by a good cooper, and this will put a bit more of the original oak taste back into the wine.

Winemakers are violently divided upon the topic of "When to put a new wine in barrel": Some advocate that a wine may be placed in barrel immediately following its first fermentation, while others insist that a wine be brilliantly clear before it is introduced to the barrel. The proponents of this school of thought believe that the gross lees are easier to clean from carboys than barrels, and that the expensive barrel will last longer if treated in this fashion. I leave the decision up to you: just remember that you must always keep your barrel filled; if not with wine, with a sulphite and water solution.

Talking Barrel Dollars

Surprise! They just aren't that expensive, especially when

you consider how many years you'll get out of them. Your barrels, whether new or reconditioned, will benefit from having their insides shaved by a cooper after a few years use. In this way, your wine will always be deriving those lovely butter-vanilla extractives from the oak.

One must be especially vigilant with barrels, for, particularly in the hotter weather, the amount of wine evaporated issubstantial. REMEMBER: If your wine ever goes "off" whilst in barrel, you have lost the barrel as well as the wine, for the porosity of the barrel can harbour bacteria that will infect any sound wine that subsequently goes into it. Just keeping it topped up avoids trouble!

Cellar Hint: | *A BARREL TRICK*

If your oak barrel is getting tired and not imparting the primary oak flavours to your wine that it used to, conventional wisdom advises to have the barrel taken apart and shaved to expose new wood. There is another option. If the barrel isn't leaking, consider using it 'as is' and adding French oak chips. I find a palmful usually does the trick, but only regular tasting will tell you. Is this cheating? You decide!

Buying Oak Barrels

While most winemakers, if asked, would prefer to buy a new oak barrel rather than a used one, new barrels are more than twice the price of used barrels. Also, not every wine can stand the stress of a new barrel: delicate reds and whites simply wither under the onslaught of all that oak!

One of the best ways to deal with new oak barrels is to put several wines "through them" in the same vintage. That is to say, you could put your biggest wine in first, a deep red Cabernet, for, say, six months. After that, two months each for the Zinfandel and Barbera. By the next vintage, the barrel will have mellowed to the point where, in the second vintage, you'll be able to leave your Cabernet in the barrel for the whole year! Buy another barrel the next year, and start the whole process over again – only this year, the other wines can wait for their chance at the new barrel while maturing in the two-year-old barrel.

The standard barrel size is 225L (50 gallons), which holds about 300 750ml bottles. This is a lot of wine, far more than many home winemakers make in a year. If you do not want to increase your production to this number of bottles, consider a half-size barrel of 110-115L (25-26 gallons), which will hold the equivalent of about 150 bottles. This is as small as you want to get. A smaller new oak barrel, even with two weeks aging, will put too much wood on the wine.

If you buy a used barrel, put your nose in the bunghole and smell. It should smell sweet and fresh, not vinegary or musty and mouldy – any "off" smells and you've just bought yourself a flower planter (better than ruining your precious wine)!

If it smells like whiskey, it's a used, knocked-down whiskey barrel and you're going to have to do a fair amount of soaking to leach the whiskey out! Even then, the first wine you put in the ex-whiskey barrel had better be a pretty gutsy red to stand up to the abuse!

Cleaning, Preparing and Conditioning Oak Barrels
For New Barrels or Second-Hand Barrels That Have Held Wine:

Fill the barrel with (preferably) hot water. Rotate the barrel so that the bung is in contact with water. By two or three days, all leaking should stop as the dry wood staves swell. If the barrel does not stop leaking with water, it will leak more with wine (which has a lower specific gravity i.e. it is less dense), so exchange it at the place of purchase, or have a cooper – good ones are few and far between – look at it.

At this point, empty the barrel, and refill it halfway with hot water and three tablespoons washing soda (soda ash) for each 40 litres (10 gallons). Dissolve the soda and add to the water in the barrel. Bung the barrel and rotate consistently (with fervour), splashing ALL of the inside (including the heads), with great intensity for at least 20 minutes. Many of the extreme tannins and oak elements will be leached from the wood during this process. Next, fill the last half of the barrel with hot water, bung and allow to stand overnight.

The next day, empty the barrel and refill it halfway with cold water, rotate vigorously as above. Empty and repeat three to four times, then fill the barrel with wine without delay.

For Second-Hand Whiskey Barrels:

First of all, smell the barrel (the whiskey aroma may knock you out, but at least it may have helped preserve the barrel from bacteria!) Shine a flashlight inside the bunghole and look for mould. If you suspect that the wine previously held in your second-hand barrel had turned, even partly, to vinegar, or there is mould present instead of bare wood, DO NOT use the barrel. Once the vinegar bacteria has permeated the pores of the barrel, any wine therein will eventually turn to vinegar.

If the barrel smells fresh and sweet, but with an alcoholic "whiskey" edge to it, follow the procedure for new barrels, but repeat the hot water procedure twice to leach out the maximum amount of "latent" whiskey possible.

As well, after the last rinse and repeat stage, if your working area allows, put a hose in the bottom of the barrel and run the water for another 1/2 hour, gently overflowing out the bunghole and down the drain.

After this labour-intensive procedure, stick your nose in the barrel and look for that sweet smell of fresh wood. The whiskey smell, once so prominent, should be greatly reduced. If not, there is no other choice but to do another series of hot water-washing soda/cold water rinses.

Using an Oak Barrel

Once your barrel is ready to receive wine, place it in a location where you want it to remain all year. The barrel, when full, will be far too heavy to move. Either make a frame, or support the sides with wedges so it cannot roll. It must be high enough off the floor so you can siphon out of it, but not too high – you must be able to siphon the wine into it (or pour the wine in through a large funnel).

The only time the barrel comes down from its perch is for cleaning.

When you have filled the barrel with wine, top it up weekly, for the wine is continually evaporating (less in winter, more in summer) through the wood staves. If there is any significant airspace above the wine, you are risking spoilage. KEEP IT TOPPED UP! Regularly remove the bung, smell the wine to see if it is developing well, and check the liquid level.

At first, fit the barrel with a fermentation lock and rubber bung. When the fermentation is truly finished, replace the fermentation lock with a silicone rubber bung with no hole in it, and give it a sharp rap with your fist (a hammer can seat the bung too tightly, making it impossible to remove) to ensure it is well-seated. These are hard to find, but well worth the search: they don't harm the edges of the bunghole. By contrast, wood and cork bungs inevitably crumble, wick up wine and promote mould, grind up the edges of your barrel's bunghole, and get pushed so far in they can't be pulled out.

| Cellar Hint: | **BOTTLING FROM THE BARREL** |

A couple of weeks before you plan to bottle, it is best to siphon the wine back into carboys, using a sulphited rag in the bunghole (or the plastic cone that comes with some siphons) to hold the siphon wand absolutely steady so as not to stir up the sediment. This gives you a chance to see the sediment level in the carboys when you are bottling to get the most limpid wine possible, something that is impossible to sdo with the opaque wooden barrel. Also, by pouring the dregs of the barrel through a funnel into a carboy (you'll need a friend to help you lift the nearly-empty barrel), a bit of extra wine can be salvaged when the muddy dregs settle.

| Cellar Hint: | **SPRAY GUN CLEANLINESS** |

Keep some sulphite solution in a window-washer-type spray bottle to ward off fruit flies and mould on the exterior of the barrel, and especially around the bunghole. Spray any affected area as often as needed. Unchecked mould can eventually work its way into the barrel.

REMEMBER: YOU MUST MAKE SUBSTANTIALLY MORE WINE THAN IS NEEDED TO FILL THE BARREL, BECAUSE YOU WILL NEED TO TOP-UP THE BARREL ALL YEAR, SOMETIMES BY AS MUCH AS A BOTTLE A WEEK IN THE WARMER WEATHER.

Storing Oak Barrels

To store an oak barrel, rinse it at least four times with cold water, IMMEDIATELY after emptying it of wine. Fill the barrel half full, and rotate it vigorously, rinse. Repeat three times. If you have access to a drain, you could leave the hose in the barrel for 15 minutes at the end for a really thorough rinse.

FILL the barrel immediately with approximately 250g (one cup) sulphite and 100g (approx) (just under 1/2 cup) citric acid for each 40 litres (10 gallons). Top up the barrel every month with cold water, and empty and repeat these steps three times a year, as long as the barrel is not filled with wine. Dissolve the sulphite and citric acid in water BEFORE you pour them into the barrel to make sure they are well-mixed.

Section IX

Bottling and Labelling

Bottling is one of the most important steps in winemaking: if done well, it ensures the safety of your wine for a long period of time. (Fig. 10, p. 120).

Labels and capsules may seem completely frivolous, having nothing to do with the quality of the finished wine, but after you have worked long and hard on your "baby," labels and capsules make your wine appealing to others – and that's a notion that should not go unconsidered.

Saving Different Bottle Types; why?

You have doubtless noticed that every time you buy a bottle of Chardonnay (or any white Burgundy), the bottle is a certain shape, and when you buy a Cabernet (or a Bordeaux), the bottle is another shape. This is no accident, but an unwritten agreement

Fig. 10

A properly filled and corked bottle with 1/2 inch of airspace.

between wine producers to standardize bottle shapes so that consumers have an idea which section of the wine store they're in without having to constantly pick up bottles and read the labels.

There are four basic types of wine bottles, and a quick trip to the wine store will fix these firmly in your mind:

1. **Dead leaf green, soft-shouldered Burgundy-shaped:** White and Red Burgundy, Chardonnay, Pinot Noir. The Loire's Chenin Blanc, the Côtes-du-Rhône and Châteauneuf-du-Pape use a darker green version of this bottle, as do some Riojas.

2. **Dark green tall-shouldered Bordeaux shaped:** Bordeaux, Cabernet Sauvignon, Zinfandel, Rioja and most other reds use this bottle, as well as some Bordeaux whites. Similar brown or dark green Bordeaux-styled bottles with a thinner neck are used for Chianti and other Italian reds.

3. **Long, angular-sloped green or brown bottles:** German white wines; Alsatian whites are in a similarly shaped bottle that is more blue-green.

4. **Clear white Bordeaux shaped: Rosé, Italian whites.**

While you are drinking commercial wine, you can be saving and sorting bottles for your homewine, and, while you're at it, why not drink the same kind of wine that you'll be making? That way, you'll have the right kind of bottles at the ready.

Recycling bottles the best way: for your wine!

If you find you can't save enough bottles from the commercial wine you buy, try asking friends and local restaurants to save them for you: after all, isn't re-use the best form of recycling?

Storing Empty Bottles

Bottles can be stored anywhere you have a little room and

some available shelving, however, shelves aren't portable, and you don't want to carry your empties, (bottle by bottle) to the sink or bathtub to wash, then to your bottling area, and, finally, back to storage. Some home winemakers like to store their empty bottles in commercial cardboard 12 bottle wine cases, but I find these take up a lot of space.

If you make your wine from grapes, save the wooden lugs that the grapes came in to store bottles! If you like the slope-shouldered Burgundy bottles, the lug will fit four rows of five, or twenty bottles. Twenty-four Bordeaux (see cellar Hint below) bottles can be stored in these boxes which can even be carried on their sides, one in each hand, the bottles fit so snugly!

I find the long Alsatian or German bottles also work well but the case must not be carried or stored on its side.

If you like the idea of using lugs but don't make your wine from grapes, simply haunt the grape markets next summer, and, when you see a big customer take 40 + cases of grapes home, ask if you can have a few empty lugs when she or he has finished with them!

Cellar Hint: THE "BORDEAUX BOTTLE TRICK"

Unlike Burgundy bottles, Bordeaux bottles interleaf nicely in a grape lug, so you can fit in a few extra: in alternating rows, you'll be able to squeeze in six X four rows (24 bottles – 2 cases of wine!). As well, if you always put the first bottle in the bottom right-hand corner of the box, you will be able to push TWO boxes together (see illustration) to make a neat, stable storage unit that's stackable (maximum three units high) to store either empty OR full bottles. You'll find this little trick looks nice, saves a lot of space, and is very practical.

Storing Filled Bottles

Burgundy Bottles

Burgundy bottles store well in quantity, when full, neck to neck, laid interlocking. This is an old Burgundian trick that has to do with the original design of the bottle. They don't have

Fig. 11

Storing bottles in grape lugs: The "Bordeaux Bottle Trick."

much space in Burgundy, and they believe they can store more wine this way.

Bordeaux Bottles

When you are storing many full-punted Bordeaux bottles, they can be laid down with the neck of the first bottle inserted into the punt of the second row, and a stable pile built that way. This then, is one of the original design reasons behind the Bordeaux punt, besides the way it traps sediment for decanting. Otherwise, use the "Bordeaux Bottle Trick" to store your wine. (Fig. 11, p. 123)

Washing and Sterilizing Bottles

If you're really the organized type, as each bottle comes into the house, you'll soak off the labels and store the bottles immediately. If you're at all like me, you'll have masses of bottles to wash just before bottling!

Fill up a bathtub or primary fermenter with scaldingly hot water and Diversol (a chlorine-based wine equipment cleaner) at the rate of about (5 gms per liter) 4 teaspoons per gallon. Using heavy plastic gloves, submerge the bottles one by one, holding them under until they sink. After a half hour, pull the bottles out.

French and Italian labels will have largely fallen off by this time. Simply rub the bottle vigorously with a plastic scouring pad to remove all traces of glue.

American, Australian, Spanish and other labels may be a bit trickier, even after the soak. Using a knife with a flat, thin, longish blade, scrape the label off and use the plastic scouring pad to remove the last bits of label and glue. If necessary, return the bottle to soak.

Once all bottles are clean take them to the sink and rinse the chlorine out with a jet of hot water. Press each bottle down on your bottle washer for two-three seconds. (Fig. 12, p. 126)

If you are planning to bottle right away, shake a little sulphite solution in the bottles, empty and fill without rinsing again.

If you are not bottling at this point, just give the inside of the bottle a good shot of hot water from the bottle washer and store.

Cellar Hint: **STERILIZING BOTTLES WITH SULPHITE SOLUTION**
When you are ready to bottle, rinse the previously cleaned bottle with a jet of hot water (see above). Then, using a funnel, fill a bottle 1/4 full with your prepared stock sulphite solution. Stick a finger or thumb in the bottle, give it a few quick shakes, and drain the solution, via the funnel, into the next bottle. As you are pouring the sulphite into the funnel, make sure to submerge the neck and lip of the bottle in the liquid swirling down the funnel for a second or so, to insure sterility.

Discard and renew the solution every 24 bottles or so. This little procedure can be very quick if you have one person rinsing bottles, and one "sulphiting." Fill the bottles with wine as soon as possible. By leaving a trace amount of sulphite solution on the wet sides of the bottle, the wine will be slightly protected from oxidation without adding significantly to the sulphite content of the wine. I find I can get away with less sulphite throughout the winemaking process because of this technique.

Last Racking; Filling the Bottles

Make sure you have not moved or racked the wine for at least two weeks before bottling to ensure the least amount of sediment possible in your wine.

The time for the final racking is when everything is ready to bottle and the bottles and all equipment have been washed and sterilized. Leave yourself lots of time – time is relative when you're bottling. This is the most careful racking you will ever do; care must be taken that the siphon hose not move – the lees (sediment) must be disturbed as little as possible.

Rack the wine, with as little aeration as possible, into a sulphited plastic fermenter or clean carboy. I prefer using carboys,

Fig. 12

Washing bottles and/or carboys with a brass bottle washer.
Expensive but indispensible!

because, although they are heavy, there is little danger of the wine spilling as you carry it; no need to cover it with a towel or plastic during the bottling; and one can see the wine level going down as the bottling proceeds, letting you know if you're running out of bottles.

Take the clean, just-racked wine to your bottling area, put it on an elevated surface like a table, arrange a suitable quantity of bottles on the floor below the carboy, start the siphon, fill the bottle to within 1/2" (1.3 cm) of where the cork will be, and voila!

You will waste much less wine if you buy an inexpensive automatic shut-off valve that fits on the bottom of your siphon hose – it will allow the wine to flow when in contact with the bottom of the bottle, but will shut off automatically when the siphon wand is lifted out of the bottle.

| Cellar Hint: | **FILLING BOTTLES ACCURATELY – AND QUICKLY**

The bottling will go a lot faster if the person filling doesn't try to get the level perfect every time, but just performs the basic filling function. Have a friend finish off the bottles perfectly using a half-full bottle of wine and a funnel. That way, bottles that are slightly high or low in the fill level can be easily and quickly levelled out to the optimum fill height. This little step saves time in the corking process. (Fig. 13, p. 128)

Driving the Cork Home

Best-quality corks are a very important link in the fine wine chain if you plan to keep your wine for any time at all. Inferior quality corks crumble, are hard to insert, and could be bad for your precious wine. Spend the buck or two extra per 100 and sleep at night!

Just before you are ready to cork, bring a covered pot of water and your corks to a boil, and let them boil furiously (top on – corks float, so that the ones on top will steam) for at least 10 minutes. Drain, rinse and return to pot and let them soak in

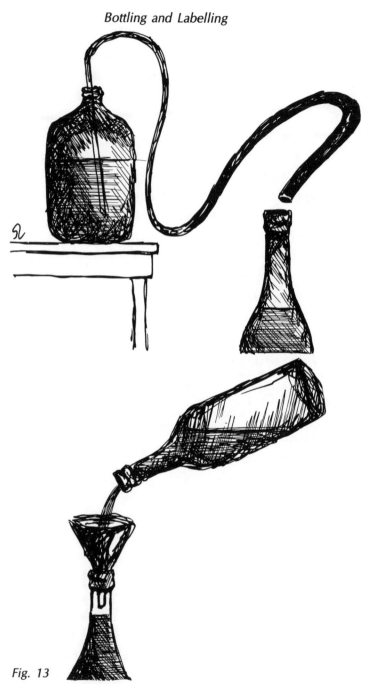

Fig. 13

Filling bottles; fine tuning is done with a sterilized funnel.

a fair amount of sulphite solution. Begin corking immediately using a hand corker (for more than 50 bottles, it gets tiring), or splurge
on a good floor corker (you will have it for many years, and so
will the next generation). In any case, you must work fairly quickly
before the soaked, pliable corks dry out.

Whichever model of corker you choose, be sure to finish
the downstroke by pulling the level up again, ready to receive
the next cork. This sounds like a trivial matter, but incorporating
this last up-stroke into your corking motion will speed and
streamline the process considerably. Stand the corked bottles up
for two days so that the outermost face of the cork will have time
to dry. If you lay the bottles down immediately, you may incur
some wine leakage. (Fig. 14, p. 130)

Make an Impression:
Designing Your Own Wine Labels

It's fine to buy pre-gummed labels from your local supply
store; they certainly come in enough variety, from Merlot to St.
Émilion, Chablis to Chardonnay. But, for some, who have spent
months lavishing care on their wine, it would be unthinkable to
taint the hand-made product of their labours by affixing a store-
bought label! No; for them, it is only fitting they decorate their
bottles with custom-made labels that say exactly what needs to
be said about their product; no more, no less.

Study Other Styles:

Before deciding on a format that you feel speaks for your
product, take the time to study the huge variety of labels from
around the wine world.

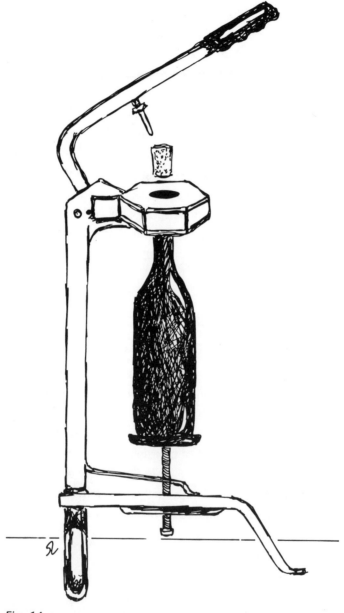

Fig. 14

Corking bottles using a stand-up or hand corker. Make sure corks are boiled and then rinsed with a sulphite solution before using.

Becoming conversant with the language of labels is a fun and worthwhile exercise. Get a good wine book with colour illustrations of labels, or go down to the biggest local wine store, look at the many varieties of wine labels, and take notes. Make sure to note the difference between inexpensive and up-market labels.

Initially, there were huge stylistic differences between the labels of Bordeaux, Burgundy, Germany and the wilder, more daring approaches of the New World, but there is now a little more cross-talk between the labels of all wine regions. Take a good look around before you decide what is best for you.

Here, then, are some classic examples:

The châteaux of Bordeaux: Typically, an elongated vertical label which complements the tall, thin bottle, and allows the consumer to read the château's name while the bottle is on the store's shelf, without having to turn the bottle. Often printed on a cream background, the typefaces are equally divided between script and serif styles. Three of the most popular type colours are black, gold and deep red. Most Bordeaux châteaux include an old-style engraving of the property's house or vineyard to lend an air of venerability and tradition to the product.

Burgundy: Most Burgundian labels are horizontally oriented, to suit the wider Burgundy bottle. The typefaces lean heavily towards script, although many types of serif fonts can be found. The Burgundians DO NOT usually put an engraving of their domaine on the label, because (unlike the Bordelais) they own small vineyards here and there, and not just in one place that can be easily pictured. There are very few "châteaux" in Burgundy anyway: most growers live in simpler homes in the villages.

Germany: The most striking features of the long German

label are the evocative, but hard-to-read Gothic script, and the sheer quantity of words, designed to help the consumer pin down the exact vineyard from whence the wine came.

United States: The most notable aspect of the American label is the willingness to experiment with new ideas. Some have been extremely well-conceived; others are unsightly abominations. Any type of image, design element, colour and typeface may be found on an American label; it seems there are no un-written rules that any particular region must follow. The old world, especially Italy, has started to take tentative steps down this new path.

Hand-Made Labels

Handmade labels are a great option if you are artistic, or have a good hand for calligraphy (or have a friend who does). With this option, your product is presented in a totally non-commercial, homemade way: each label is an original work of art. However, if you have more than 25-50 bottles to label, it can become a little tedious, to say the least. If you want to go this route, read on anyway: you may be able to incorporate some of the design techniques and artistic layout ideas that follow into your hand-made labels.

Design Basics for Photocopied/Printed Labels
Label Size

Personally, I like to use a label size that will work with all my bottles, from my whites in Burgundy bottles that call for a horizontal label, to the reds that go mostly in Bordeaux bottles, which usually look better with a vertical label. I find that 11cm x 10cm (roughly 4 1/4″ x 4″) is pretty well the optimum size if you want to make one label that will look well on most size bottles. The back label, if any, should not exceed 7.5cm X 10cm (about 3″ x 4″).

Another, labour saving idea is to make a wrap-around label that combines the front label with a side label, instead of a separate back label. Lots less hassle to glue! See Ridge and/or Dry Creek Vineyards of California for good examples of this concept. Some Italian companies also take this tack.

| *Cellar Hint:* | **THE "BACK LABEL TRICK"** |

Rather than making five different labels for all the different types of wine you make, simply make one front label with no indication of grape type, just your "domaine's" name and the year, and include the wine type information on the one common back label used for all the wines. Code your wines by capsule colour and bottle shape. For example, the coding part of your back label could read something like this:

- Loire-style Chenin Blanc: Burgundy bottle, white capsule.
- Barrel-aged Chardonnay: Burgundy bottle, yellow capsule.
- Cabernet Sauvignon: punted Bordeaux bottle, red capsule.
- Zinfandel: flat-bottomed Bordeaux bottle, green capsule.

Because printing costs per label go down the more you print, by taking this approach you can have a good-looking label for all your products, yet still tell the individual wine's story on the back.

Typeface

Once you have decided on the size of your label, the next hurdle is designing and setting the type. Although you can pay your printer to typeset your copy, you will probably not get the attention to detail and typeface selection you'll need to turn out a first class label.

Letraset (and other press-to-apply lettering)

An inexpensive way to see your "Château Moi" in print

is to make an original with Letraset, (letter transfer sheets available at graphic design stores in major cities) but make sure to draw light pencil lines to guide you. These can be erased later when the job is complete. Bring patience and a steady hand – and watch the spacing of the characters carefully: they must be evenly spaced to the extent that it looks natural to the eye. Remember: a poor Letraset job looks worse than good handwriting.

Letraset and its competitors also make a variety of line tapes, which will enable you to make decorative boxes around the text, artwork, or borders around the label itself. One or two closely-spaced thin lines is perhaps the most elegant arrangement; certainly, this approach has stood the test of time!

Typesetting

Professional typesetting houses, although they deliver the goods, can cost you a lot of money, if you must use one, go in with your lettering design drawn out exactly to size, and let them suggest several typefaces from which you can choose. Consider taking along a commercial label to show the typesetter the kind of typeface you'd like to emulate. Make sure to tell them what kind of box you'd like: they can do it!

Personal Computers with Laser Printers

If you can avail yourself of a word-processing system (like *WordPerfect*) on a P.C. with a laser printer and a decent selection of typefaces and sizes, you'll be able to come up with a pretty good-looking label.

However, don't try to do your whole label, artwork included, on a P.C. unless you have a state-of-the-art desktop publishing system (and know how to operate it well). Otherwise, you may produce a label with a less than elegant "computery" look.

If you can't create boxes on your P.C., consider line tape (see the paragraph on Letraset).

Layout Basics

Printers require what is called "camera-ready-artwork" from which to reproduce your label. Paste your border lines and text on bright white cardboard exactly as you wish it to appear. If you are simply photocopying your label, any illustration you use should be simple line art. If you want to use a photo, have a commercial typesetting house make a "photostat" (not to be confused with a photocopy) or "half-tone" of the photograph, and this will reproduce somewhat better.

Commercial printers can handle shades of grey and reproduce colour tints in black and white with little problem, so you can be more creative where illustrations are concerned.

If you will be printing your label, put a correctly-sized photocopy of the illustration in place, and inscribe the words "For Position Only" on it in marker. Give the original to the printers, and have them shrink it down to size. By writing on the photocopy, you allow them to see the placement you want, but they will not be able to print it by mistake with the words "For Position Only" on it.

Make sure to indicate, on a tracing paper overlay you have taped to the board, how much of a border you'd like the printer to leave around your box, if any (I find a 6mm – 1/4" trim is classy).

Colour should also be indicated on the overlay with coloured pencils or markers.

Choosing Your Paper Stock

At your printers or photocopier's ask to see a good selection of suitable paper. Make sure not to go with something too thin (looks cheap!) or a paper too heavy (pulls off the bottle when glued). Texture gives an interesting effect; if you can get a lightly ribbed or parchment-like cream paper, it can look very authentic.

Make sure to choose a pale, lighter colour for your paper, darker colours will obscure the print and art.

Two and Three Colour Printing

If you have a lot of bottles to label, you may be able to justify the extra cost of an extra colour on your label. Ask your printer for details. Besides black, deep red and gold leaf are the most common colours used, They seem to denote a certain richness, implying that the wine in the bottle is very good! Very dark brown is an excellent replacement for black, and, when printed on cream paper, can have a subtle, warming, harmonious effect.

Cellar Hint:	**MY ETHNIC PRINTERS**

When looking for printers in bigger cities, don't overlook any small, often ethnic, neighbourhood printers. If they are printing pizza flyers by the million, you've got the right place. The job you get here may cost as little as one third what a bigger company will charge you, but be careful of the quality. Try corner-store stationers and photocopy shops too.

Sticking the Labels On

Over the years, I've tried just about every way of gluing labels on: glue stick (not bad, but tedious), roll on glue (wrinkly), white glue (aaaagh!), and now, finally, I've discovered spray adhesives. They are a pleasure to work with, IF you have a well-ventilated space. The 3M Company makes a good one that remains tacky for a long time, letting you spray a a good number at once, but it is expensive.

Positioning Your Labels

When you are studying labels in the wine store, note label placement: the Italians and Americans are particularly inventive here, getting a "designer" feel by using all sorts of high and low placement the French would never consider. Get creative – and get some friends to help you – just make sure to show them one perfect bottle as an example!

Choosing the Right Capsule

It's your wine. Choose any fanciful colour you want to complement the colour of your wine, label colour(s) and bottle, but, if you are trying to be authentic in your reproduction of certain styles of wine, this short list will help you identify some of the colours commonly used in the traditional wine regions.

Burgundy and Beaujolais:
Red Wines: bright red and Burgundy red are traditional.
White wines: yellow is traditional, white also used.
Bordeaux:
Red Wines: a bright red or deep red/maroon, or
metallic Bordeaux colour, but black is also common.
White Wines: white/cream, yellow or gold.
Sweet Sauternes-like whites: gold.
Italy: black or maroon are often used, sometimes metallic red or royal blue.

Cellar Hint: If you have a hankering for real lead/tin foil capsules, I suggest you inquire at wineries in your region, or in regions you visit while vacationing. I once got some beautiful burgundy and yellow-coloured lead capsules from winemakers' supply stores while on vacation in Beaujolais and Burgundy. Look for the handy little plastic form that pushes them over the bottle top, too, because you can never get a perfectly smooth job doing it by hand.

P.S. Don't worry about the lead and your health; although the media often plays up stories about lead capsules being potentially dangerous, if you strip away the lip of the capsule and wipe the spout before pouring, there will be no contamination of the wine. In any case, most capsules of this type will probably be tin, or some tin alloy in the near future.

"Shrink-Wrapping" Plastic Capsules

This is one of the easiest and most satisfying parts of being a winemaker. Bring a tea kettle of water to a furious boil; meanwhile, put the case of just-corked wine on a table next to the stove. Drop the capsules loosely on the tops of the bottle. Once the water is boiling dip the top of the bottle into the path of the steam, or the boiling water itself, holding the capsule on with a long-handled perforated stainless steel spoon. You will be amazed how quickly the capsule heat-shrinks to the bottle neck, making a perfect fit. Return the bottle to the case and continue. That's all there is to it! Just make sure to leave the bottle standing up for a day or two until the outermost face of the cork dries.

Section X

Some Thoughts On Cellaring Your Wine

One subject that is not often spoken of is the aging of home-made wine; do they have the capability to improve with age? Section 8 covered the maturation of wine, which we'll define as the "growing up" of wine until it is bottled in its early adulthood. (The French literally call this period "élévage"). The aging of wine, then, is the time the wine spends in bottle before it is drunk.

Despite some big wine corporations' efforts to the contrary, wine is a living substance, that continues to evolve (not always for the better) in the bottle.

For this evolution to take place, you must lay your bottles down sideways, so that the cork is kept wet by the wine, and will not shrink, thus making an effective barrier to the air.

Situating Your Cellar

The fantasy: envision the mythical "European cellar:" a damp, dark, cool place with rows upon rows of cobwebby treasures sleeping patiently on their sides awaiting their eventual call to the dinner table.

The reality: many modern wine drinkers live in apartment complexes, condominiums, townhouses, flats and even country cottages that have little access to the subterranean.

Defining a European-Style Cellar

Historically, cellars may have been the repository of wine more by default than by choice, but, neatly, they are also the ideal storage place, for they are: 1. spacious and handy; 2. dark, (ultra-violet rays are harmful to wine); 3. stable in temperature: 13°C (55°F), more or less, throughout the hot summers and cold winters; 4. sufficiently humid to prevent the corks from drying out (some call it damp!); and 5. vibration-free.

Another one of the beautiful aspects of the classic European cellar is the temperature. In the winter, whites can be brought up at a moment's notice, and they will be at the perfect temperature to serve. In the summer, bring up a bottle of red on the hottest day of July, and it too will be at the perfect temperature for serving. If (coming back to the real world) your dwelling is quite warm in the summer, and you wish to prevent reds from tasting "soupy," you may have to put them in the 'fridge for 15 minutes, or run them under cool water. This will take the edge of warmth off without "chilling" them.

Using this "European cellar" as a model, we can now determine how best to establish our "home cellars:" let's look at all of the modern options to see how they fare in comparison.

Taking Your Temperature

Seen by many to be the biggest problem facing the "Home Cellar," temperature, in most cases, is of little consequence. Aside from excessively high or low temperatures, wine will age with no ill effect in temperatures ranging from 0° to 24°C (32° – 75°F), although the ideal range is between 10° to 14°C (50° – 57°F). The main thing to avoid, in any situation where wine is being stored, is a rapid temperature swing from cool to hot.

The average city dwelling will hover at 20°C (68°F) most of the year, edging up a few notches as the summer progresses, but this is gradual, and will not affect the aging process. It is always a good precaution, however, to keep the whites closest to the floor where it is coolest, for they are the first to suffer from "heat exhaustion."

Humidity

The question still lingers: "Does the aging of wine in a consistently "warm" household speed up the maturation process; have no effect; or is it detrimental to the wine?" Many authorities claim it hastens the process, others claim it has a negligible effect. It seems no one has ever cared enough to set up a long-term experiment! At higher temperatures, whites do seem to deteriorate faster than long-term reds, but even reds will deteriorate if the corks dry out because of a lack of humidity, causing evaporation through the cork, and "ullage" (lower bottle fill height that may lead to premature aging due to the increased presence of oxygen in the bottle).

Based on this, one could then safely set up a primarily-red wine cellar (with some whites for short-term drinking) with no worry about the temperature being constantly above the ideal.

Getting Into Closets

A closet, preferably a walk-in closet, is one of the best places in which to establish a "home cellar" – but it must be reserved solely for the use of wine, as constant disturbance to "get a towel" or "a pair of boots" defeats the purpose.

A closet is handy, dark, vibration-free, and relatively stable in temperature throughout the year, making it pretty close to the ideal. If your building experiences large temperature swings, you might want to install a purpose-built refrigeration system (most major wine accessory shops will sell these units) in the closet, to control the temperature AND humidity. The space must then also be insulated to prevent the unit from running constantly. The unit will have to be vented through a wall into an adjoining room, so this is not a good option for those who rent and cannot modify their space.

If your closet has no refrigeration unit, ventilation holes should be drilled or cut into the door to keep the air fresh, and at the same temperature as the rest of the house. Beware of central heating and/or hot water pipes in the walls!

Note: Most closets will work best with upright bottle racks, which can be ordered or assembled to custom fit. The main function of a rack, no matter how sophisticated or simple, is to keep the bottles stored on their sides, so that the cork will remain moist from contact with the wine, and, hence, impenetrable to air.

Cellar Hint: **THE "ROTATING ICE BLOCK" TECHNIQUE**
For those who would like a cooler, more humid closet without the expense of installing and running a cooling unit, here is a simple technique: freeze two four-litre (one gallon) plastic ice cream containers full of water. Place one at the bottom of your closet, and leave the other in the freezer. Exchange the two containers of ice every morning, and, depending on the size of the closet, you will be able to maintain a temperature of 16°-18° (60-62°F) at all times. If the cupboard is kept full of wine, the liquid in the bottles will contribute to maintaining a stable temperature.

With the 'Rotating Ice Block' technique, it is of paramount importance that the cupboard not be opened more than once a day, to conserve the cool temperature.

You must take out any wines you will need for the day in the morning when you switch containers, and forbid anyone else in the household to open the closet!

Converting the Junk Room or Spare Bedroom

If you have a small room at your disposal that is presently collecting rummage, you may have just stumbled on a neat alternative to an underground cellar. A room, however small, offers the kind of luxury that comes from having a bit of space, and you will be able to decorate it like a wine cellar, complete with an area to decant over a candle, perhaps even installing a small desk and chair for keeping records.

The room can be fitted with a combination of bins (for your larger, long-term lots of wine) and single-bottle racks, for the odd lots and ready-to-drink wines.

To keep the room dark, the door will have to be closed at all times, and the windows covered, so it would be wise to provide for ventilation, whether through holes, a grate in the door, or by other means.

If the room has a separate thermostat, all the better for guarding against winter overheating. If the room has a window as well, you could consider running a small air conditioner in the summer, which, with judicious use of the thermostat in winter, would have you within the 'ideal' temperature range all year 'round! Be careful, though, if you are considering storing high-priced wines for really long (20 years +) aging. Air conditioners can make the air dry, which may lead to the corks drying out.

In The Kitchen or Under The Sink

These are popular choices but they should not be. The combination of temperature changes due to cooking and water pipes, and the constant vibration of kitchen traffic make this a poor choice for anything but the shortest term storage.

Under The Stairs

If the stairs themselves are really solid and cause no vibration, this is a viable option, equally as good as a closet or room, except that you will not be able to hook up a cooling system (should that be your desire) without building an enclosure.

Instant Cellars: A Viable Option?

If none of the above options are realistic because of space or other considerations, there is always the deluxe route - buy an "instant" wine cellar!

There are some remarkably sophisticated "Refrigerated Wine Storage Units" on the market, which come in an array of sizes and finishes from handcrafted wood (for the armoire look) to glossy ultra-violet-filtered black lucite (to show off your treasures without opening the door). These are free-standing enclosures that are intended to be beautiful pieces of furniture that will enhance your decor, rather than detract from it. Made in a variety of sizes that hold from 40 to 350 bottles, they are the ultimate in condo wine care.

Before buying, however, the home winemaker would do best to consider the cost of aging wine in this fashion. Add the cost of the unit and the running costs in electricity per year together, then divide by the bottle capacity of the unit. Add the figure on to the average price of a bottle of your wine. Is the wine worth it? The decision is yours.

A Cellar In The Basement?

How novel! If you do have a bit of basement space, but it is finished and/or heated, there is an option: Modular Wine Rooms! These are a similar concept to the "assemble your own Sauna" – "assemble your own furniture" products, except that they are wine cellars complete with cooling systems. They are an affordable alternative to designing and doing it yourself! Most start at a basic 500-700-bottle size.

Installing Wine Racks and Bins

No matter what your cellar arrangements, it is always better if the shelves or racks are installed with a one-sixteenth to a maximum of one-half an inch of slope to the rear, to ensure that any precipitated sediment will settle towards the bottom of the bottle. As well, at this angle, the cork will still remain covered by the wine.

A Cool Warning

Despite all their elegance and convenience, it must be remembered that any refrigerated wine storage is a luxury, and not a prerequisite to "cellaring" wine. Any budding home winemaker wishing to start a cellar should do so immediately – at room temperature, in the best location you have at the moment! There is no time like the present to begin – let the refrigeration come later, when space and the pocketbook permit!

Bottle Age: you'll never have fine wine if you always drink it the first year!

Wine lovers generally like a well-aged wine. Yet, home

winemakers, even when they are knowledgable wine lovers, tend to bubble over in their enthusiasm (excuse the pun) and pop their corks too soon.

Bouquet and Aroma

In a tasting of store-bought wines, if a wine lover should bring up the difference between "bouquet" and "aroma," he or she is thought pedantic, a snob, or, at the very least, a nit-picker! For home winemakers, the difference is crucial!

Let's take a look at the definition of these terms, taken from Peter Schaffter's glossary in "For the Love of Wine", Kylix Media Inc., 1990: Aroma ...the odour of grapes or fruit in a wine. (grapiness) Bouquet ...all the odours present in a wine that are not directly attributable to grapes.

To illustrate the point, let's use a 100% Cabernet Sauvignon wine, a classic Bordeaux-style wine many North Americans make with grapes from California, Washington, Oregon, New York, Maryland, Texas, the Virginias, and, increasingly, British Columbia and Niagara.

Directly after vinification (fermentation), the new wine abounds with yeasty, fruity grape aromas. A few months later, the nose is decidedly more vinous, but the grapiness remains. This kind of fresh grape aroma is often referred to as "primary fruit" in wine-tasters' notes. Young Beaujolais smells this way, as do many wines from the Midi. You might call this the "aroma stage" of the young wine.

By the six to nine month point, the watershed is reached: the wine finally has "bouquet!" Depending on the source wine region, vintage, condition, and vinification of the grapes, the wine will start to shed its grapiness, and start to exhibit odours that, if not yet complex, seem to suggest other fruits. At this stage in a Cabernet wine, cherries, blackberries, black cherries, black raspberries, stewed plums, prunes and "red cough drop" fruit may now be discernible.

Were a winemaker to consume all of his or her wine by a half a year after the vintage, the bouquet wouldn't have had a chance to develop.

Between the first and second year, the wine ceases to be a gawky, pimply teenager and becomes a confident young adult. In our Cabernet example, cassis, butterscotch/vanilla (from wood aging), tobacco, leather, chocolate, coffee, spice, herbal and numerous other olfactory sensations will (hopefully) start to clamour for your attention! By the time your home wine reaches this point, it should be bottled, to preserve the fruit, so that the woodsy, leathery and tobacco components don't predominate.

But What does it Taste Like?

By the time your "nose" comes into line, the taste of the wine should follow. From the embryonic, grapey-fresh fruit and tannic bite of the initial wine, a magical transformation will take place: the mouth will seem to come together, the tannin drops off, the wine softens, and is more "balanced." The fruit and acid have come into line. The grapey taste is replaced by the more complex, mingled fruits, etc., and (best-case scenario) a tantalizingly-long finish.

Determining your "Drinkability Window"

The "window," or time frame, in which you drink your wine will be largely a matter of personal taste, but it is my experience that most people prefer their wines just before they cease to evolve: it's the time when the best compromise is reached between fruit, complexity, and drinkability. This will vary from grape to grape, but most sturdy reds aren't at their best for two to five years. If that sounds like an awfully, awfully, long time, take heart: you don't have to save all your wine, just some of it! Hey! Half the fun is getting there! (Make notes on the way, though - you'll be smarter next time!)

On one hand, there are many people who prefer the juicy fruitiness of their wine when it has just been bottled, while others insist on 10 years of mellowing - minimum - for all their reds. To each her or his own!

The Age of Commercial Wine

Let's face it, basic Beaujolais aside, even cheapo red commercial wines are released in their second year! Classic wines, like those from Bordeaux, Burgundy, California, and the better wines of Italy are not released until their third year, at least; with Spanish Reserva Riojas, and Italian Barolos being famous for their late (5 + years) release dates.

If you're the type who likes to surprise friends by pretending your wine is commercial wine, or to compare your bottle against the world; at least give it a chance by giving it a little age.

Section XI

Other Techniques:

Sparkling Wines:
Three Techniques for Making Your Own
"Méthode Champenoise" Without Sediment

A Sparkling Discovery: The Champagne "Expulsion Cap"

Anyone who can make a still white wine can make a "Champagne"-style wine with ease.

A sweeping statement? Not really. While the variables in winemaking in general are great, those in *mousseux*-making are far more controlled. Basically, it's a re-fermentation of a still wine – and it all happens in the bottle, so, once the wine has re-fermented, the hurdle is getting the yeast sediment out of the bottle!

But, that's a bit ahead of the story here; let's take a closer look at how to get the wine to sparkle, and then we'll follow up on the yeast-ridding process.

A Description of the Méthode Champenoise:

Méthode champenoise is the original name of the classic method used in Champagne for centuries. (Outside Champagne, the process must now be called *Méthode Traditionnelle* by EEC rules). The Champenoise guard their appellation ferociously, and for good reason: they've had to fight off imposters (old world and new) for ages. *Méthode traditionnelle*, then, refers to the re-fermenting of a still wine IN the bottle.

To proceed, start a wine from grapes, juice or concentrate in the late fall. Test for acidity: wines that are already low in acid are not recommended for sparkling wine; the refermentation process eats up a bit more acid, risking a lifeless, flabby, couch-potato-of-a-wine! The best pre-sparkling wines are well-structured, fresh, varietally pure whites with a decently "big" mouthfeel. Chardonnay is a favourite, so is Pinot Blanc (Pinot Gris would be great), but I also like Chenin Blanc. Very defined varietals, like Sauvignon Blanc, are less likely to please in bubbly form.

Once your still wine has reached a fair degree of clarity naturally, say, late February/early March, bottle the wine in sturdy, thick Champagne bottles (you might have to drink the real stuff just to get the bottles!), adding some Champagne yeast and a measured amount of sugar (usually, 1-1/2 ounces of granulated sugar per gallon or about 45 gms per 4 litres of wine to be sparkled) and cork.

Although the still wine was previously dry, the added sugar gives the yeast something to work on, to ferment to produce the much desired CO_2.

The fact that this wonderful miracle of the Lawrence Welk "Tiny Bubbles" all happens in a sealed bottle means that the wine retains the CO_2 produced in a dissolved form, and, once the bottle is opened – "pop!" – the wine has a sparkle!

There is also a little extra – ahem – alcohol produced as a by-product of the re-fermentation, so the ideal candidate for the sparkling process would be a still white of 11°. In fact, if you start with a very alcoholic wine of 13.5° or so, it is likely that the Champagne yeasts will die off before doing their job of sparkling the wine, and you'll end up with a flat, artificially-sweetened wine! So make sure that your base wine is low alcohol, high-acid.

Once the sugar has been added, and the cap tied down, keep the bottle in a warm environment, shaking up the yeast every day or so for the first few months. After this time, the fermentation should be complete, but the wine will benefit from continued exposure to the yeast for up to a year. A periodic shaking of the bottle (daily at the beginning) will distribute the complex yeast essences and allow the wine to re-ferment evenly. Remember, the yeast must circulate throughout the wine at this stage. It is only at the end that we invert the bottle and riddle the yeast down onto the cap.

Getting the Yeast out of the Mousseux: Three Approaches

What's not so simple is the age-old problem of getting rid of the spent-yeast lees that form as a by-product of this fermentation.

Once the wine has cleared (after about six to 12 months in bottle), the corked bottle is put upside-down in a specially designed rack (or whatever contrivance you come up with), and "riddled," which means the bottle is turned a quarter-turn every day until the wine clears and the yeast settles firmly on the bottle cap.

Once that goal is attained, we need to get the yeast out of the throat of the bottle – but how?

A. Dégorgement

The most traditional approach: the neck is frozen (the CO_2 escapes less at low temperatures), the bottlecap removed, and a plug of frozen yeast is ejected (Fig 15a). The wine is topped up with a dosage or *liqueur d'expédition* of sugar/still wine, depending on the desired style (brut to dry), and is recorked with a protective wire basket. Presto! Clean, clear wine!

Degree of difficulty for first-timers: **Herculean!**

B. The Champagne Expulsion Cap!

Hark! Have we finally an answer to the age-old riddle? The Champagne Expulsion Cap (Fig 15b), when I stumbled across this gadget earlier this year, seemed to be the "no muss, no fuss" solution to the problem. What I loved about this method is that the bottle never needs to be frozen! As well, the cork doesn't need to be exchanged – the Expulsion Cap is the same size as a traditional Champagne cork, and fits under those nice foil capsules you can buy at any homewine store.

Here's how it works: When bottling, cork with the plastic "Expulsion Cap." Proceed as for *dégorgement*, except, instead of removing the cork to disgorge, pull on the tiny ripcord. The pressure inside the bottle will force the quantity of yeast out of the bottle, and into the sink. When you are sure the yeast is gone, tilt the bottle back upright, chill and serve! With the "Expulsion Cap," no need to disgorge until the day you are serving the wine!

If, however, you feel the wine has had enough exposure to the yeast and you wish to disgorge them all, great! Especially if you intend to keep the wines awhile, in which case it would be best to top up the bottles with a "liqueur d'expedition." Chill the clear bottles (just disgorged) in the 'fridge for a day (or freezer, but watch it!) – any angle is o.k. – to lower the bottle's pressure. Take off the cork, taking care not to shake the bottle, and pour in the dosage. Replace the "Expulsion Cap" with a regular plastic Champagne cork and wire down.

Degree of difficulty for first-timers: **A Snap!**

C. The Nipple Method

This method works much the same as the "Expulsion Cap," except that the yeast is collected in a plastic nipple of the cap that is exterior to the bottle (Fig 15c). When the wine is clear and has the right pressure, the plastic is firm to the touch, like a bike tire. It is then gingerly bent as you right the bottle and the bent nipple full of yeast sediment is wired to the now-clear bottle.

Degree of difficulty for first-timers: **Fairly Difficult**

If you care about your wine's appearance at all, the cork must be changed!

How my Expulsion Cap Misfired

It is always important to understand traditional *dégorgement* (disgorgement). Once, when I was testing the "Expulsion Cap," a bit of yeast was not expelled but stuck on the lip of the cap in the bottle, just enough to muddy my perfectly clean wine had I righted the bottle. To correct this I placed the bottle, still upside-down, in the freezer, after which I disgorged the wine in the traditional manner with a flick of my baby finger. (Remember to measure the inside height of the freezer before you buy your next fridge!)

Fig. 15

**Three sparkling wine (mousseux) stoppers
on the market.**

Fig. 15a

Regular Cork (neck must be frozen and
sediment disgorged in the classic
méthode Champenoise).

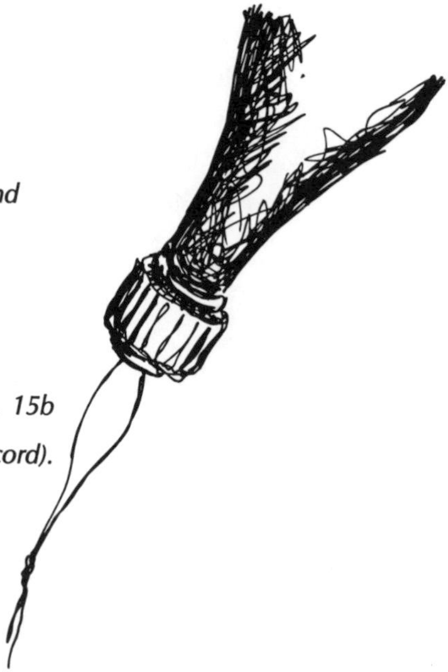

Fig. 15b

"Expulsion Cap" (just pull the ripcord).

Fig. 15c

The Nipple Method. The nipple
collects the sediment while the bottle
is inverted, then, as the bottle is
righted, the nipple containing the
sediment is bent and secured to the
side of the bottle. Presto! Clear wine!

Rosé Wine

To make a rosé, simply press the red grapes immediately, as you would with a white wine. If you wish the colour a little deeper than a "blush," simply leave the grapes to macerate for a short time. Experience will tell you which varieties work best, and how long to leave them to macerate, but great rosés have been made from Grenache, Cabernet Sauvignon, Zinfandel ("White Zin"), Cinsault, Carignan and even Pinot Noir!

Once the wine is pressed, return the press wine to the free-run and simply treat it as you would any white wine (to avoid oxidation) throughout the fermentation, maturation and bottling.

Experiment and have fun!

| *Cellar Hint:* | **CONCENTRATE YOUR RED WINE BY MAKING A ROSÉ!** |

Once the skins have macerated with the must for a short while, draw off roughly one third of the total batch as free run and ferment. The French call this process a *saignée* or "bleeding" of the must. The balance of the must and skins will now make a bigger, more concentrated wine than would have otherwise been possible! This is a great technique for making deep red wine in poor years – and the rosé is a bonus!

Dessert Wines

Since yeast slows down/dies off at alcohol concentrations between 14-15 per cent, it follows that natural sweet wines can be made when the amount of sugar in the must exceeds the ability of the yeast to ferment it.

This can be attained by using very sweet late-harvest grapes, or by drying (as in Italy) the grapes on straw mats to concentrate the sugars by evaporating the water.

In practice, grapes need to attain levels of at least 26° Brix to be suitable for sweet winemaking. One can try to ferment to 14 per cent alcohol, but most winemakers ferment the must as usual, and when the fermentation slows down (at 12-13 per cent alcohol), the wine is racked and given three times its normal dose of SO_2 - 6 grams of sodium metabisulphate for 19 litres (a heaping teaspoon for 5 gallons). This stops further fermentation, kills or immobilizes the yeast, and protects the wine from nasty bacteria. When the wine has settled further, it is racked again, with a similar addition of sulphite, to separate the wine from the yeast and bacteria A.S.A.P.! The winemaker must add SO_2 at every racking (in the normal amounts) from then on, to protect the wine from the dangers of refermentation.

Try using ultra-ripe California Sauvignon Blanc, Muscat, or Sémillon for this purpose.

A Mega-Sulphite Alternative

Commercial wineries, to avoid using all this extra sulphite, often chill the wine to 0°C (32°F) and centrifuge when they want the fermentation to stop. As this is not practical for the home winemaker who does not want to over-sulphite, the most realistic course to take would be to let the fermentation finish naturally (this may take till the spring), then add some Süssreserve (sweet reserve of grape juice) back to the finished wine (late spring-early summer), sulphite, let marry, then bottle.

The "Buddy System"

As with any endeavour in life, sharing the ups and the downs makes them a lot more tolerable. When you group together as a unit of four or so to make wine, costs are reduced, and purchasing power is increased. Where a single winemaker might not have the resources, initiative or space to get into winemaking alone, the physical, financial and moral support of others can be key to getting the effort off the ground.

A friend of mine, Ian Curtin, leader of one such "Buddy System" in Victoria, B.C., believes that the unit of four is the perfect number for making wine. The group splits the cost of a crusher, press, primary fermenters, and four oak barrels at the outset, having only to split the cost of grapes in successive years.

Singly, one would have to buy all the same equipment, buying one oak barrel instead of four. In addition, the four share the winemaking responsibilities at the crush and throughout the year, meeting at two week intervals. If one or two of the members are not available, two can easily carry out the routine maintenance and racking. After bottling, each member of the Victoria "Buddy System" cellars at least 200 bottles of premium wine a year, at a very reasonable cost-per-bottle.

Section XII

The World of Wine

Classic Wine Regions of the World and their Grape Types

Whether you're into making wines from concentrate kits, fresh juices or grapes, you'll be better able to decipher the world of home winemaking if you approach the subject from a commercial wine standpoint.

YOU may drink nothing but home wine, but understanding the wine world will give you a solid base upon which to build. Some commercial wines are named after CLASSIC WINE REGIONS, while others are labelled by GRAPE TYPE. Understanding which grapes the classic wine regions use (but don't necessarily indicate on their labels) is part of the key to being able to replicate their style of wine, even if you don't buy much commercial wine.

The only thread that ties the world of wine styles together is grape varieties, or varietals, as they are called. Once you know the predominant grape variety of any region, you need not be intimidated by "château" and producer names – even the most expensive "Pommard" will be "Pinot Noir" to you, and the greatest, most expensive Bordeaux château will be simplified to being a mixture of mainly Cabernet Sauvignon and Merlot.

Buying Juice and Concentrate Kits

Many juice and concentrate kits come with a place name (the name of a classic wine region), rather than a grape name. Following this paragraph there is a handy list of some of the renowned regions of the world and their *encépagement* (grape varieties the region is planted to) that you are likely to see on a home winemaking kit's label. Home winemakers working from juices, concentrates, or even directly from grapes can use this list to buy separate varietals which can be then blended to approximate the blends of well-known wine regions.

Where more than one grape type is listed, the first variety named usually predominates in the blend, and the other varieties decrease in importance as you descend the list.

France
Bordeaux Red is a blend of: Cabernet Sauvignon, Merlot, Cabernet Franc, Petit Verdot

Other Communes Making *Red Bordeaux* (Bordeaux Rouge) That You May See On A Label: Médoc, Graves, St. Julien, Pauillac, Margaux, St. Éstephe

St. Émilion (Libourne region in greater Bordeaux area)

A blend of: Merlot, Cabernet Franc, Malbec, Cabernet Sauvignon

Pomerol and *Fronsac* (Libourne region in greater Bordeaux area – same as above)

White Bordeaux (Bordeaux Blanc) is a blend of: Sauvignon Blanc, Sémillon, Muscadelle

Other Communes Making *White Bordeaux* That You May See On A Label: Entre-Deux-Mers, White Graves

Sauternes (Sweet Bordeaux white) is a blend of: Sémillon, Sauvignon Blanc, Muscadelle

Alsace – these varieties are NOT blended, but bottled separately: Pinot Blanc (Pinot Bianco in Italy), Tokay/Pinot Gris (Pinot Grigio in Italy), Riesling, Gewürztraminer, Sylvaner

Burgundy (Red): 100 per cent Pinot Noir

Other Villages Making Red Burgundy That You May See On A Label: (All should be 100 per cent Pinot Noir) Pommard, Gevrey-Chambertin, Chambertin, Nuits-St. Georges, Aloxe-Corton, Beaune, Côte-de-Beaune, Côte-de-Nuits

Burgundy (White): 100 per cent Chardonnay

Other Villages Making *White Burgundy* That You May See On A Label: (All should be 100 per cent Chardonnay) Chablis, Meursault, Montrachet, Puligny-Montrachet, Corton-Charlemagne, Mâcon, Mâcon-Villages, Pouilly-Fuissé, St. Véran, Beaujolais Blanc

Muscadet (Loire): Muscadet. Sometimes called Melon de

Bourgogne. (Muscat is another spicier, grapey variety grown in most countries, including France, that is not to be confused with Muscadet.)

Hermitage (in Northern Rhône): 100 per cent Syrah ("Hermitage" of Australia is Shiraz = Syrah)

Côtes-du-Rhône is a blend of: Grenache, Carignan, Syrah, Mourvèdre, Cinsault, and many more

Châteauneuf-du-Pape is a blend of: Grenache, Syrah, Mourvèdre (Mataro in Australia), Cinsault, (and 9 others!)

Italy
Chianti is a blend of: Sangiovese, Canaiolo, Mammolo, (and others). *Brunello di Montalcino*, and *Vino Nobile di Montepulciano* are also Sangiovese-based.

Barolo and *Barbaresco*: 100 per cent Nebbiolo

Valpolicella and *Bardolino* are a blend of mostly: Corvina, with the possible addition of some: Rondinella, Molinara, Negrara, Rossignola. (Also permitted, in small quantities: Barbera, Sangiovese, Garganega)

Soave is a blend of: Garganega (minimum 70 per cent), Trebbiano (maximum 30 per cent).

Spain
Rioja is a blend of: Garnacha (Grenache), Tempranillo, Graciano

Germany
Niersteiner, Mosel, Hock, Piesporter, Rhine, Rheinhessen, Rhe-

ingau, Rheinpfalz, etc. are all place names that may use any of the following grapes, depending on the quality of the product; Riesling (the most noble), Müller-Thurgau or Silvaner.

Any of the approved German grapes are permitted in the production of Liebfraumilch: however, Liebfraumilch is almost always made from Müller-Thurgau and Silvaner, Riesling being too expensive.

Grape Types for North American Winemakers

By the time harvest season comes around, keen home winemakers have already decided how deeply to commit to winemaking for the year. By late August, most of us have saved, begged or borrowed enough capital to get our feet really purple!

The list that follows was conceived expressly with the North American home winemaker in mind; it is a compendium of the most prevalent grape varieties that are available in the various grape-growing corners of our continent, compiled so that the home winemaker can do some advance research before the harvest.

I have not included information on native North American vines or their crossings, because I have not had the pleasure of tasting their wines, or working with them. I have, however, included many of the French-American hybrids.

The area where the grape first came to prominence is in parentheses after the grape name. Each entry includes a "General Comments" category, as well as one on "Flavour Characteristics" (i.e. please bear in mind not all wines labelled say, "Merlot," necessarily taste exactly like the description, but this is what is expected from that grape, depending on where and how they are grown).

Red Grape Varieties

ALICANTE-BOUCHET (France) (Vinifera Crossing, Grenache X Petit Bouschet)
GENERAL COMMENTS: A "teinturier" grape (literally, a "dyeing" grape) which is one of the few to have red pulp as well as a red skin. Makes intense, dark purplish wines whose colour drops out quickly, often within two years or so. Planted extensively in California's Central Valley and still favoured by the ethnic market to make "drink within the year" wine. Shipped to larger cities all across the United States and Canada.
FLAVOUR CHARACTERISTICS: Fairly neutral wine, flabby, and only useful when deep colour is needed – for a short time.

BACO NOIR (French-American Hybrid, Baco no.1, Folle Blanche X unknown Riparia)
GENERAL COMMENTS: Some say that Cabernet Sauvignon genes lurk somewhere in the parentage of Baco Noir. Certainly, the reds are quite dark, and the grape is said to have been crossed near Bordeaux...
FLAVOUR CHARACTERISTICS: Deep red wines, sometimes mute but correct bouquet. Sometimes neutral, but hearty and smooth mouthfeel after a few years aging. One of the best hybrids.

BARBERA (Piedmont) (Vinifera)
GENERAL COMMENTS: Barbera is Dolcetto's competitor for the most-regularly drunk, daily red in Piedmont, but, unlike Dolcetto, Barbera has managed to widen its sphere of influence considerably. Shipped from the Central Valley of California, where most of it is grown, it makes a bland, medium coloured, but usefully acidic addition to commercial jug wines – and home winemakers' blends – all across the continent. It will be interesting to watch the cooler areas of California to see if Barbera carves out a real place for itself, or remains a blending grape.
FLAVOUR CHARACTERISTICS: Deep purple wines with a high level of zippy acidity on the finish. It enjoys a popularity among those who drink it young, and also among those who like to treat it to a little wood aging (chestnut casks are traditional, but oak is more common today) and see it mature into something a little more refined.

CABERNET FRANC (The Loire & Bordeaux) (Vinifera)
GENERAL COMMENTS: In the Médoc, the Cabernet Franc is generally thought of as a blending foil for Cabernet Sauvignon, but in other areas, because it ripens earlier than Cabernet Sauvignon, it often is used as a substitute. It is an important variety in the Libourne district (St.-Émilion, Pomerol and Fronsac) because of this. Where the Cabernet Sauvignon would have trouble ripening, Cabernet Franc is used to blend with Merlot, bringing many Cabernet Sauvignon qualities to the finished wine. Hence, it is not a "lesser" cousin, but a useful alternative, and unfortunately hard for home winemakers to find. Most wineries treasure Cabernet Franc as a blending grape, so there is not much on the market. Being grown in Washington, British Columbia, Ontario, New York State, as well as (of course) California.
FLAVOUR CHARACTERISTICS: Remarkably similar to Cabernet Sauvignon, but lighter in colour, and body. Slightly more herbaceous than Cabernet Sauvignon, the wines also have an approachable "juiciness" and a lower level of tannin that makes them easier to quaff.

CABERNET SAUVIGNON (Bordeaux) (Vinifera)
GENERAL COMMENTS: Cabernet Sauvignon is considered to be the most classic grape variety by many, and not just because it's the famous grape of Bordeaux. Cabernet Sauvignon is famous because it transplants so well, making wines of good structure and class in many viticultural regions. The combination of thick skin and small berries gives a concentration of aroma, flavour, colour and fruitiness simply not found in most grapes. To compound this, the Cabernet Sauvignon is naturally a low yielder, which only concentrates the flavours more. The breeding of this vine is such, that even a small addition improves a blend – a true thoroughbred, but the best are slow to mature.
FLAVOUR CHARACTERISTICS: Deeply coloured wines of good balance, great Cabernet Sauvignon have bouquets that reveal traces of cassis, blackberry, mint (California), cigar box, cedar, butterscotch, green peppers, chocolate, cocoa, leather, etc. A great wine will often have a deep, plummy richness on the nose that prefigures the actual taste of the wine. Most good "Cabernet Sauvignons" will be full-bodied, showing an intense fruitiness, acidity and astringency in the mouth when young, but mellow with time to become rich and sinful – yet still bone dry. Of course, Central Valley Cabs display less class than this, but still manage to be mouthfilling.

CARIGNAN (Southern France) Vinifera)
GENERAL COMMENTS: One of the most important grapes in the Rhône, Châteauneuf-du-Pape, and France's Midi, also grown widely in California, especially, the Lodi region and the Central valley. Brings some class to jug wine blends.
FLAVOUR CHARACTERISTICS: Good grapey, juicy fruit. Responds well to partial Maceration Carbonique. More alcohol and less taste when it comes from the Central Valley of California. Medium tannin.

CARNELIAN (California) (Vinifera Crossing Cabernet Sauvignon X Carignan X Grenache)
GENERAL COMMENTS: Affordable hot country hybrid of Cabernet Sauvignon X Carignan X Grenache, bred to an elegant Cabernet-like vine in the scorching San Joaquin Valley (Central Valley).
FLAVOUR CHARACTERISTICS: Good colour. Decent, plummy mouthfeel that can taste pruney in the hot years.

CHAMBOURCIN (French-American Hybrid, Johannes-Seyve 26205)
GENERAL COMMENTS: Rhône valley origin, fairly widespread plantings in North America, as well as the western Loire in France.
FLAVOUR CHARACTERISTICS: Ordinary wine, but deeply coloured with a fairly robust flavour and mouthfeel. Can age.

CHANCELLOR (French-American Hybrid, Seibel 7053)
GENERAL COMMENTS: The parentage is said to contain Alicante and Cabernet Sauvignon genes, and it originated in the Rhône valley. A parent of Villard Noir.
FLAVOUR CHARACTERISTICS: A well-coloured, ageable, medium-bodied red of some bouquet and elegance.

CHELOIS (French-American Hybrid, Seibel 10878)
GENERAL COMMENTS: Has not fared as well as some of its contemporaries, but is nevertheless popular in New York State, Idaho and Washington, as well as the mid-west.
FLAVOUR CHARACTERISTICS: At its best, a well-coloured, quite decent, "poor man's Burgundy."

CINSAULT (Southern France) (Vinifera)
GENERAL COMMENTS: Popular in the Rhône and in the south of France, some sources indicate it is called Black Malvoisie in California. Inexpensive.
FLAVOUR CHARACTERISTICS: Fruity, soft wine. Fun to try partial Maceration Carbonique with, or blend with Carignan and Grenache to make a Rhône-styled wine. Dark in colour, even from hot climates, unless the yields are too high. Good, meaty (if rustic) blending grape. Low tannin.

DE CHAUNAC (French-American Hybrid, Seibel 9549)
GENERAL COMMENTS: Hardy variety planted mostly in B.C.'s Okanagan, Ontario; the U.S. Midwest, New York State and the northeast.
FLAVOUR CHARACTERISTICS: Reliable cool climate variety, has been reasonably successful. Good fruit and balance.

GRENACHE/GARNACHA (The Southern Rhône/Spain) (Vinifera)
GENERAL COMMENTS: Grenache is fabled for the oceans of fabulously fruity rosé wine it makes all over the vinous world, due to its light pink skin. What most people don't know is that Grenache can be a kind of chameleon, making

purplish, concentrated wines from older vines if planted in a cooler microclimate and the yields are kept low. On arid plains, like those in the Midi of France and the Lodi Valley of California, the productivity and sugar levels soar, resulting in high alcohol wines that often have the flavour baked right out of them. On the positive side, Garnacha-influenced Riojas are some of Spain's classiest reds. It is a major ingredient in the Châteauneuf-du-Pape cocktail, and Château Rayas, one of the best Châteauneuf-du-Papes, is nothing but! Grenache figures prominently in all of the southern Rhône reds. After Shiraz, Grenache is Australia's second most widely-planted red grape variety, but it is rarely bottled as a varietal.

FLAVOUR CHARACTERISTICS: Cherry. Many Rhône wines will exhibit a cherry colour in the glass, a cherry nose, and a cherry attack in the mouth. In tastings, even those who disagree with the use of the word "cherry" will invariably detect "red fruit" in the nose and the mouth. The more concentrated Grenaches, if they have been treated to a little wood aging, have an unctuous, buttery-spicy fruitiness that is almost sweet (but totally dry to the taste). The other giveaway is the Grenache body, which, without being "big" in the classic, concentrated sense, has a smoothness and thick unctuousness that belies its lighter colour.

GAMAY (Gamay Noir à Jus Blanc – Beaujolais) (Vinifera)
GENERAL COMMENTS: THE grape of Beaujolais, where 98 per cent of the red grapes planted are Gamay. A wonderful grape that captures the bacchanalian spirit of the harvest in all its grapey glory! Beaujolais is best in the year after the harvest, so it's a pity that all the grapes going into Nouveau Beaujolais are not making sturdy, juicy, standard Beaujolais. Beaujolais Nouveau is a wonderful harvest celebration, but it should not be the only type of Beaujolais we drink. Perhaps if we were not drinking so much Nouveau, we'd be better able to discover the everyday pleasures of having a solid Beaujolais on our table! It is very hard to find the real thing in North America. (Ontario and British Columbia have some plantings.)

FLAVOUR CHARACTERISTICS: It is often said that Beaujolais is the purplest of wines, and while this may be true, the giveaway is the blue tinge the purple has: this is young wine! On the nose, the alluring grapey aroma of new wine (maceration carbonique – love it or hate it – see glossary), the quaffable, medium-bodied, fruity mouthfeel, and the apparent lack of tannin are the clues that will pin down the taste of Beaujolais.

Gamay Beaujolais (France-California) (Vinifera)
GENERAL COMMENTS: Not Gamay, but a poor clone of Pinot Noir making passable wine in California.
FLAVOUR CHARACTERISTICS: Vinified as if it was really Gamay.

Napa Gamay (California) (Vinifera)
GENERAL COMMENTS: Not Gamay, but the Valdiguié of the Midi.
FLAVOUR CHARACTERISTICS: Light coloured, low alcohol. Often vinified as if it was Gamay.

LEON MILLOT (French-American Hybrid, Kuhlmann 194-2)
GENERAL COMMENTS: High acidity, slightly earlier maturing, yet less widespread in North America than brother Maréchal Foch. Also planted in England.
FLAVOUR CHARACTERISTICS: Deeper coloured than Maréchal Foch, to which it is thought to be as good or superior.

MARÉCHAL-FOCH (French-American Hybrid, Kuhlmann 188-2, Rupestris X Riparia X Goldriesling)
GENERAL COMMENTS: Short-season variety crossed in Alsace, grown mostly in Ontario, but throughout the United States as well. Serviceable, but not the best of the hybrids.
FLAVOUR CHARACTERISTICS: Inoffensive, high acid, Burgundy-like in texture and lightness, colour, but no "magic."

MERLOT (Bordeaux) (Vinifera)
GENERAL COMMENTS: Every wine text points out the absolute quality of Merlot by underlining the fact that Château Pétrus of Pomerol (Bordeaux's most expensive wine) is made from nearly 100 per cent Merlot. While this is true, the Merlot is more generally prized for its ability to harmonize with Cabernet Sauvignon. This "little blackbird" is, contrary to popular belief, the most widely planted red grape in Bordeaux. From that point of view, it is Merlot that defines Bordeaux, not Cabernet Sauvignon! It may be that the top communes of the Médoc (Margaux, Paulliac, St. Julien, St. Estèphe, Graves, Moulis) use more Cabernet Sauvignon than Merlot, however, it is in the ocean of regular A.C. Bordeaux that Merlot predominates. Merlot is popular among producers for its productivity, and the fact that it does well in clay, where Cabernet Sauvignon doesn't. It also ripens a little earlier, and, in poor years, often accounts for a higher proportion of the Bordeaux blend. Washington, California, and New York's North Fork of Long Island are making strong bids to become the U.S.'s "Merlot States," but Virginia also has healthy plantings. In Canada, Niagara and the Okanagan have significant plantings.
FLAVOUR CHARACTERISTICS: Merlot can produce supple and well-coloured wines that exhibit a rich nutmeg and barnyard (a slightly rotten, funky, gamey, earthy smell) plummy fruitiness. Merlot is typified by its beguiling fruit, early softness, apparent sweetness, spiciness, and significant tannins, yet its roundness makes it fit for early drinking.

MISSION (California/Europe) (Vinifera)
GENERAL COMMENTS: One of the first grapes grown in California.
FLAVOUR CHARACTERISTICS: Rustic minor grape that produces a light-coloured wine. Not without interest, but hardly a complex, long aging wine.

PINOT NOIR (Burgundy) (Vinifera)
GENERAL COMMENTS: So many pay lip service to the great Pinot Noir (Burgundy), yet so few drink it regularly. The area Burgundy covers is so small, and

the grape so hopelessly capricious that the best will forever be priced beyond the everyday reach of all but the most well-heeled wine lovers. Yet, at its best, it is sublime.

FLAVOUR CHARACTERISTICS: It is relatively easy to pin down most of the complex nuances of Cabernet Sauvignon, but the best Pinots are ineffable, completely defying description. The only way to grapple with the complexity of Pinot Noir is to taste it. Pinot Noir can be a very dark burgundy colour, with age it is more often a deep red, but it is almost never opaque. A good Burgundy has a nose redolent of raspberries, strawberries, (red berries, not the black fruit of Cabernet Sauvignon) a slight touch of vanilla from the wood perhaps, with a certain magic soul-thrilling *"je ne sais quoi"* that will have you dreaming of the vineyards of Bourgogne. Easy to drink from the word 'go,' Pinot Noir never smells nor tastes "too" young, in the way that Cabernet Sauvignon does, it merely gets more heavenly with time. Rich and velvety at its best, Pinot Noir is also rich in contradictions; a hint of sweetness yet totally dry; somehow thinner in the mouth than Bordeaux, yet just as full-bodied; a suggestion of earthiness amidst the elegance; as it ages, less like the original fruit, and more like some ethereal heavenly nectar; this is the enigma of Great Pinot Noir.

But Caveat Emptor (buyer – and winemaker beware), the previous tasting remarks describe a "good" Pinot Noir, which is a lot harder to come by than a good Cabernet Sauvignon. No grape disappoints more people more often than the intermittently excellent Pinot Noir.

PETITE SIRAH (France) (Vinifera)
GENERAL COMMENTS: Obscure Southern French grape (the Durif) elevated to cult status in California. Not related to Syrah or Shiraz.
FLAVOUR CHARACTERISTICS: Deep-coloured and jammy with good acid; rather better than most people – including Jancis Robinson ("Vines, Grapes and Wines..." See Bibliography) – would let on. Many examples of "old vines," barrel-aged Petite Syrah can be quite firm, with good dense fruit. It is the nose and finish – but not the fruit or mouthfeel – that make it, perhaps, less complex than some of the other noble red varieties.

RUBY CABERNET (California) (Vinifera Crossing: Carignan X Cabernet Sauvignon)
GENERAL COMMENTS: Developed in 1948 at the University of California (Davis) to combine the style of Cabernet Sauvignon with the prolificacy of Carignan.
FLAVOUR CHARACTERISTICS: In the finished wine, the Carignan dominates and the wines are deep-coloured and pleasant, but, especially from the Central Valley, more Carignan than Cabernet: they do not age beyond five years or so.

SANGIOVESE (Tuscany) (Vinifera)
GENERAL COMMENTS: This very noble grape is left off "Classic Grape" lists with disconcerting regularity. Sangiovese is one of the two top grapes of Italy, but its image suffers from a huge variance in quality: poor producers sometimes make oxidized wines that are too light, with an overly acidic finish that only underlines the absence of fruit.

More plantings of Sangiovese are coming "on line" in the U.S., but it is doubtful if these will be available to home winemakers for some time.

FLAVOUR CHARACTERISTICS: Medium cherry red, often darker, with a garnet-orange rim, the Sangiovese hallmark is red fruit and berries. The suggestion of acidity, and raspberry-cherry, raisiny fruit on the nose follows through to the mouth. There is often a thin spot on the mid-palate, but the wine finishes rustically solid and chunky, with a characteristically dry, slightly bitter, acidic finish that, once recognized, is a dead giveaway of its origin.

SYRAH (The Northern Rhône) (Vinifera)

GENERAL COMMENTS: Thought by many to be one of the three greatest grape varieties of France, with Pinot Noir and Cabernet Sauvignon, the Syrah is "the" grape of the northern Rhône, where it reaches its apogée. Some very interesting wines are also coming out of Australia. Commonly thought to come from the city of Shiraz in ancient Persia, the grape was well-established in the Rhône by the time the Romans arrived. More plantings of Syrah are coming "on line" in the U.S., but it is doubtful if these will be available to home winemakers for some time.

FLAVOUR CHARACTERISTICS: Deep, dark, opaque, burnt purple to the eye, the nose of young Syrah wines are intensely spicy, often complex blends of spice, burnt rubber, burnt bakelite, tar, and strong, jammy, new wine overtones. In the mouth, the peppery-rich, sun-twanged flavours are a dead giveaway for tasters, with the best offering a claret-like concentration with age. (In fact, before the advent of the Appellation Contrôlée laws, Hermitage, a Syrah wine of the northern Rhône, was often used to improve Bordeaux in poor years).

VILLARD NOIR (French-American Hybrid, Seyve-Villard 18315)

GENERAL COMMENTS: Grown in the middle states and the southwest, as well as Canada. Chancellor is one of its parents.

FLAVOUR CHARACTERISTICS: Deeply-coloured, good alcohol, well-balanced wine that is said to have retained a touch too much "North American" flavour.

ZINFANDEL (California) (Vinifera)

GENERAL COMMENTS: Believed to be imported by the thousands of cuttings to California long ago by Count Agoston Haraszthy, Zinfandel is made in a variety of ways, from "blush" to "lush!" It may be the "Primitivo" of southern Apulia in Italy, but the more rustic and often sweet wine there does not offer much basis for comparison. So, it is the wine that California can call its own, and producers, struggling to define their image with the omnipresent Cabernet Sauvignon, now often find it easier to carve out a market niche with a meticulously-made "Zin."

Some of the hugest examples of Zinfandel can be overdone, with the fruit flavours so concentrated and focused they resemble iodine! The best producers seem to straddle a style that falls somewhere between elegant claret and the massive spicy character of the biggest Rhône wines.

FLAVOUR CHARACTERISTICS: A deep red-purple colour; there is a certain warm berry-like, jammy-intense, spicy characteristic to Zinfandel that is quite easy to pin down (once you've tasted enough of it!). There is also an ever-so-slightly acidic, fruit finish to Zin that you will come to recognise with time. Warm is a key word with this big friendly bear of a wine.

White Grape Varieties

AUXERROIS (Burgundy, France) (Vinifera)
GENERAL COMMENTS: An ancient Burgundian vine, in many ways similar to Chardonnay.
FLAVOUR CHARACTERISTICS: Perfumed, light, fruity wines that are best grown in areas too cool for Chardonnay. Can be quite elegant.

BACCHUS (Germany) (Vinifera Crossing, Silvaner X Riesling X Müller-Thurgau)
GENERAL COMMENTS: Another of the manifold Riesling/Silvaner crosses, this one has the added twist that it incorporates Müller-Thurgau into the blend.
FLAVOUR CHARACTERISTICS: Light, grapey wines which have considerable elegance of bouquet and good acidity. Develops with bottle age.

CHARDONNAY (Burgundy) (Vinifera)
GENERAL COMMENTS: Were this a popularity contest, Chardonnay would undoubtedly be listed first. Chardonnay, THE legendary white grape of Burgundy, has pervaded every corner of the vinous world. Unlike its red partner, Pinot Noir, Chardonnay is easy to grow, and flourishes virtually anywhere grapes can be grown. No doubt about it, Chardonnay is, singly, the best-known grape on the planet right now (red or white), partly because it tastes so good, partly because of marketing and the trend towards white wines, and, partly because the name, Chardonnay, is so pronounceable that anyone can sound like a wine snob! Almost every wine region in North America grows the grape!
FLAVOUR CHARACTERISTICS: People regard Chardonnay as an instantly recognizable variety, and yet, it has no tell-tale aroma that is "patently Chardon-

nay," as Riesling, Gewürztraminer, and Sauvignon Blanc have. What Chardonnay does have is a capability to age, a full body, and a facility to absorb flavours, responding to different winemaking techniques: some winemakers ferment in small barrels, others in stainless steel, and some will use small barrels only for aging. Some winemakers employ pre-fermentation maceration on the skins, while others will press the juice from the grapes straight away, discarding the skins immediately. Some prefer to stir up the lees during aging, to promote a certain complexity. Most winemakers who oak their Chardonnay have experimented with the type of oak used: French Limousin, Allier, Nevers or American, and even the degree of toasting (charring by fire) inside the barrels. All of these techniques leave their imprint on the resulting wine, to say nothing of the "terroir" of the growing site, and, hence, around the world, people find a large spectrum of flavours in different bottles of Chardonnay, from the unripe to tropically overripe. Ripe apples; pineapples; mangoes; oriental fruit; pears; peaches; melons; vanilla; butter; caramel; green flavours; steeliness; slate and flintiness are all descriptions frequently used at Chardonnay tastings.

CHENIN BLANC (The Loire) (Vinifera)
GENERAL COMMENTS: At its best only in the Loire, where it can be coaxed to make a number of different styles of wine. In some regions of California, winemakers take nearly three times the quantity of grapes off the same acreage as do the vintners in the Loire!
FLAVOUR CHARACTERISTICS: Without stretching the comparison too far, the Chenin Blanc plays a similar role in France to the Riesling in Germany: it has an appley-honeyed-floral scent, tart acidity and good weight in the mouth. It is made in styles that range from bone dry to pleasantly apéritif sweet to unctuous, noble-rot influenced nectars. In California, increasingly, the variety is being used as a "fighting varietal" these days, now that Chardonnay has become too expensive, making a thirst-quenching, lemony-yeasty wine of some richness that must be drunk young.

EHRENFELSER (Germany) (Vinifera Crossing, Riesling X Silvaner)
GENERAL COMMENTS: Another Riesling X Silvaner cross, this one produces wine worthy of the Riesling, yet it ripens two weeks before Riesling.
FLAVOUR CHARACTERISTICS: Riesling-like, with less intensity, but nevertheless can make wines of some distinction.

FRENCH COLOMBARD (France) (Vinifera)
GENERAL COMMENTS: In France, it is a rather unimportant third-string Cognac grape known as Colombard, while in California, it is the state's most-planted wine grape (the more planted Thompson Seedless is a table grape often used for wine) currently much-used as a bulk blender to add class to jug wines in California.
FLAVOUR CHARACTERISTICS: Can make a lemony, correct wine that should be consumed in its first year to conserve freshness.

GEWÜRZTRAMINER (Germany) (Vinifera)
GENERAL COMMENTS: Gewürztraminer is good for the ego. If you taste one good example of Gewürz, you'll never forget it. Gewürztraminer is so recognizable that you'll be able to pick it out from a flight of six others at the second tasting. "Gewürz" is German for "spice." Being grown with success in Washington, as well as Niagara and the Okanagan Valley in British Columbia.
FLAVOUR CHARACTERISTICS: "You'll love it or hate it." So goes the traditional wisdom about Gewürz, a grape so pungently perfumed with flowers and spicy-tropical fruits that you are convinced it will be sweet as sin when you taste it! You'll be surprised, however! In the mouth, the wine is often bone-dry, attractively spicy, full-bodied and elegant with a discernible finish of dried rose petals! Not a wine that is easily forgotten. The skins of the grape are slightly pigmented, and the resulting wine is one of the deepest coloured whites, often with a discernibly pink hue.

MÜLLER-THURGAU (Germany) (Vinifera or Vinifera Crossing)
GENERAL COMMENTS: One of the world's most widely-known crossings (supposedly Riesling x Silvaner, but more probably one clone of Riesling crossed with another), Muller-Thurgau was first identified and used in 1882 as part of the never-ending search for a more prolific and earlier-ripening Riesling taste-alike. Unfortunately, although it does ripen earlier, it does not taste very much like Riesling. Its presence in the Mosel somewhat debases the reputation of the region, but is understandable from the point of view of the grower weary of waiting for the tardy Riesling to ripen. It provides the backbone for many a Liebfraumilch blend.
FLAVOUR CHARACTERISTICS: Much less exciting than Riesling, but serviceable. Usually medium dry, with less acid than the Riesling, not long lived. Rather short on the nose, with sometimes a hint of muscat, the best examples can nonetheless aspire to be very pleasant and palatable apéritif wines.

MUSCAT OF ALEXANDRIA (Greece, Italy, France, Spain... which of these Mediterranean nations had it first?)
GENERAL COMMENTS: Not as noble as the Muscat Blanc à Petits Grains, it is nevertheless much more widely planted, with small pockets being grown all over the world, including California.
FLAVOUR CHARACTERISTICS: Grapey wine with a distinctive, musky aroma. Not as good for dessert wines as the more noble Muscat Blanc à Petits Grains.

PALOMINO (Spain) (Vinifera)
GENERAL COMMENTS: One of THE Sherry grapes of Xeres, grown in the merciless heat of California.
FLAVOUR CHARACTERISTICS: Soft flabby wine of limited interest.

PINOT BLANC (Burgundy) (Vinifera)
GENERAL COMMENTS: Pinot Blanc is a descendant/mutation of Pinot Noir,

and not of Chardonnay, as many enthusiasts believe. Because of its lower sugar, greater production, and vague varietal definition, Pinot Blanc is used more and more often for "bubbly" production, but its real vocation is as a still elegant wine. Grown mostly in Coastal California, Oregon, Washington, B.C., and Niagara.

FLAVOUR CHARACTERISTICS: Not very aromatic, but fresh, interesting, mouthfilling and somewhat more viscous than the legions of other light whites on the market. Pinot Blanc is often seen as a cheaper alternative to Chardonnay, and certainly, if it had the wood aging it is rarely treated to, it would be a lot harder to tell the difference. As it is, it makes an elegant but soft white with good extract that does not have the staying power to age more than a few years.

RIESLING (The Rhine) (Vinifera)

GENERAL COMMENTS: Before you say: "I don't like sweet German wines" take a moment to come to grips with the Riesling, one of the world's most noble grapes. Any grape that captivates the hearts and souls of all the best winemakers in all of Germany's vine growing regions has to have something going for it! The key: the grape has good acidity, so whether the wine is sweet or dry, it always finishes on a crisp note. Riesling is subtly complex, elegant, in a refined, European sort of way. Try: Niagara, B.C.'s Okanagan, New York, and Washington State.

FLAVOUR CHARACTERISTICS: Ah, the nose! Soft, yet strong; perfumed nuances of peaches, apricots, lemons, honey, and the somewhat startling smell of petrol as it ages. This is a wine you can come home to. Give Riesling a second chance, no, a third, fourth and fifth chance, and you will surely come to love the subtle complexity of the grape. It is not overwhelming with strong primary smells, but the bouquet's layers emerge and unfold with each sip of the wine. The wines are made in trocken (or dry) styles, right up the ladder to wines so unctuously sweet that they are the very nectar of the gods. One can imagine this wine being poured by Cherubim into Bacchus' waiting cup!

SAUVIGNON BLANC (The Loire & Bordeaux) (Vinifera)

GENERAL COMMENTS: People are often introduced to Sauvignon Blanc through Bordeaux Blanc, which is a Sauvignon-Sémillon blend, but the best varietal definition comes from the Loire, especially from the Sancerre and Pouilly-Fumé appellations. Some of the better Bordeaux châteaux are making interesting dry white wines, but the middle palate of these is often fleshed out by Sémillon. Sauvignon Blanc is also an important part of the sweet white wines of Bordeaux, such as Barsac and Sauternes, where it is blended in, again with Sémillon, for aroma and to add extra acidity.

In the early 1970s, Robert Mondavi of Napa, California devised an effective way to sell Sauvignon Blanc: age it in barrel to add "toastiness," and rechristen it "Fumé Blanc." The idea caught on, and it was explained that the barrels approximated the "flinty-fumé" character of the wine of Pouilly-Fumé. This was not strictly true, as Loire Sauvignons develop their flintiness from the terroir (see

Glossary), and not from wood, but who wants to spoil a good story? (People often confuse the Sauvignon-based Pouilly-Fumé of the Loire with the Chardonnay-based Pouilly-Fuissé of Burgundy. Just remember that Pouilly Fumé is like Mondavi's Fumé Blanc: they're both Sauvignons.)

FLAVOUR CHARACTERISTICS: Usually a very light yellow in colour, almost a light green, the wine has a "grassy" herbaceous cat's-pee nose that telegraphs the acid you will be shortly tasting, to your brain. The attack is all apples and lemons and citrus fruits, but not overly so, more bracing than puckering. The further south this grape is grown, the less pronounced the acidity, and the more evident the grassy/herbal/basil characteristics.

SÉMILLON (Bordeaux) (Vinifera)

GENERAL COMMENTS: Nowhere else in the agricultural world is the presence of mould (Botrytis Cinerea) more prized than in Bordeaux. This "Noble Rot" (which does not occur every year) attacks the Sémillon late in the growing season, shrivels the grapes, concentrating the juice, and eventually produces a heavenly nectar that commands equally celestial prices.

DRY Sémillon is increasingly produced in Bordeaux, sometimes with the use of oak barrels and extended maceration of the skins. Some say that Bordeaux is taking its cue from Australia, which has been marketing Sémillon as a dry varietal for many years!

FLAVOUR CHARACTERISTICS: When tasting sweet Sémillon, such as Sauternes or the late harvest Sémillons from Australia and California, it pays to remember that much of the aroma is in fact attributable to the "Noble Rot", and not the grape itself. Unctuous, ultra-rich, concentrated, yet possessing a highly acid structure, these wines are meant to be sipped and savoured, as they have a length in the mouth that other wines envy. Note the difference in the New World examples, where the fruits are indefinably tropical, acidity is less predominant, and spicy new wood plays a much bigger role.

Dry Sémillons have a broad feeling in mid-palate, and usually some herbal spiciness. Provided the acid levels are decent, this can be a very enjoyable style of wine.

SEYVAL BLANC (French-American Hybrid, Seyve-Villard 5246)

GENERAL COMMENTS: This crossing is being marketed as a varietal wine in Canada and the United States with some success. Grows well in cooler areas.
FLAVOUR CHARACTERISTICS: Makes a light pleasant, refreshing, green-apple tinged wine with a pleasing herbaceousness. Clean aroma. Best examples are not unlike a Muscadet.

VIDAL BLANC (French-American Hybrid, Vidal 256)

GENERAL COMMENTS: Cold-climate grape grown with success on both sides of the Canadian-American border. Has Trebbiano (Ugni Blanc) in its parentage.
FLAVOUR CHARACTERISTICS: Decent aroma, light, delicate wine – some feel it is superior to Seyval Blanc.

Section XIII

A Word on Wine Disorders

It may seem like a tired discourse to continually harp upon the importance of cleanliness, but the fact remains that all wine disorders are preventable, with the exception of those brought on by old age. A regular regime of hot water and Diversol (a chlorine-based cleanser) with regular sulphite solution rinses will avoid most problems.

A cool cellar is also a great help to keeping bacteria away. If your wine is sweltering at 33°C (90F°) all summer, you are going to be more prone to infections, as well as rapid aging.

For biological problems like mycoderma; "Flowers of Wine" (Flor); "ropiness"; acetobacter (acetic fermentation = vinegar); other anaerobic bacteria; or a mouldy taste from a mouldy barrel – if they are detected in time, you may get away with a good dose of sulphite, and a racking the day after.

Chemical problems, like ercaptans, or hydrogen sulphide's patented "rotten eggs" smell, or "yeast autolysis," an overbearing 'off' yeasty smell that comes from the wine spending too much time on the lees, can be gotten rid of by a few good rackings with aeration – IF you detect it early enough.

I find the treatments many writers propose worse than the problem; if sulphiting and racking won't solve the problem, the best advice I can give you is to throw the batch out (spoiled wine just tastes and looks awful – but it shouldn't hurt you, by the way): you'll be a little wiser – and cleaner – the next time.

Acknowledgments and Dedications

I would like to thank Kylix Media Inc. for allowing me to rework and reprint several tracts from my first book, written with Barbara Leslie (and others) entitled: *For The Love Of Wine*.

I must also thank *Wine Tidings* Magazine for allowing me to rework and reprint various portions of the homewine columns I have written over the years. If I saw something I thought was a particularly good turn of phrase, or a topic that was already well-expressed in a column, I saw no reason not to include segments of it here. I am not one for needlessly reinventing the wheel, but I will rebuild it!

A Dedication:

To Ronald Bachelder, my brother, who bought me my first homewine kit... would all this have happened if not for that fateful Christmas morn? What a long, strange, interesting ride it's been!

I would also like to make a further dedication to Mary Monica Delaney, who has helped me every step of the way through years of arduous home winemaking grunt-work (and made it even more fun!), and to all the friends who have given so freely of their time to make the dream, that is each year's vintage, come true.

A special thank-you must go to the Delaney family, who were always ready to lend a hand when there were dirty jobs to be done, like washing and scraping the labels off 400 bottles, or lending cars to pick up crazy quantities of grapes!

I'd like to publicly acknowledge and thank the gang at Shefford, who have been so supportive, and particularly the people at Kylix: Barbara Leslie, for being there to exchange ideas with, and her tireless editing of my always-too-long writing style; Linda Connors, for her good humour and world-class graphic design ideas, Russell Proulx, for his great photography and purple hands at vintage time; Mary Sambrook, for her proofreading and excellent Index; Trevor Rochester and Michael Blakely for their message-taking, plant watering and comic relief; Lucy Rodrigues and her Accounting Dept. for you-know-what; Willow Young-Codner, for the cheddar-cheese popcorn (no preservatives) and all her meticulous typesetting and John Sambrook, for the encouragement, wine + tasting expertise, good ideas and room-to-move he's given me over the years.

Of course, I must mention that Judy Rochester is the dynamo without whom none of this would have ever been possible: she had the idea, she pushed it (and me) along in so many ways that I would not be writing these words now had she not existed!

The last dedication, must go to all the home winemakers of the world, past and present: the people – let's not forget – who ORIGINATED winemaking all those millennia ago, and who remain at the heart of it still.

The biggest commercial winemaking enterprises will come and go, but small-scale winemakers will ever vinify bravely on... As long as there is fruit to ferment, home winemakers will ferment it! This book is for you.

Thomas Bachelder
Montréal, July 1992.

BIBLIOGRAGHY

Anderson, Burton. *The Wine Atlas of Italy and Traveller's Guide to the Vineyards*. London: Mitchell Beazley, 1990.

Anderson, Stanley F. with Hull, Raymond. *The Art of Making Wine*. New York: Hawthorn/Dutton, 1970.

Bachelder, Thomas and Leslie, Barbara. *For the Love of Wine*. Montréal: Kylix Media Inc., 1990.

Cadieu, Paul. *Lexiwine* (Wine Dictionary). Pernand-Vergelesses, France: Paul Cadieu, 1987.

Cox, Jeff. *From Vines to Wines*. Pownal, Vermont: Storey Communications Inc, 1988.

Duncan, Peter and Acton, Bryan. *Progressive Winemaking*. Andover, Hants, Great Britain: The Amateur Winemaker Publications Ltd., 1984

Gulling, Rich and Vargas, Pattie. *Country Wines*. Pownal, Vermont: Storey Communications Inc, 1992.

Jackson, David and Schuster, Danny. *The Production of Grapes & Wine in Cool Climates*. Wellington, New Zealand: Butterworths Horticultural Books, 1987.

Jean, Paul Jr. (editor-in-chief). *Better Winemaking*. Nepean, Ontario: Various issues through 1990/1991/1992.

Johnson, Hugh. *The World Atlas of Wine*. London: Mitchell Beazley, 1985

Johnson, Hugh. *Vintage: The Story of Wine*. New York: Simon and Schuster, 1989

Lichine, Alexis. *Alexis Lichine's New Encyclopedia of Wines and Spirits*. New York: Borzoi, Alfred A. Knopf, 1984.

Leslie, Barbara (editor). *Wine Tidings*. Montréal: Kylix Media Inc., Various issues.

Masson, Georges. *Wine From Ontario Grapes: A Guide to Winemaking with the New Hybrids.* Niagara-On-The-Lake, Ontario: G. Masson, 1979

Papazian, Charlie. *The Complete Joy of Home Brewing.* New York: Avon Books, 1984

Pellegrini, Angelo M. *Lean Years, Happy Years.* Seattle: Madrona Publishers, 1983.

Power, Keith and Joyce. *The Wine Cellar Manual.* Mill Valley, CA.: PDS Publications, 1991.

Robinson, Jancis. *Masterglass – A Practical Course in Tasting Wine.* London: Pan Books, 1983.

Robinson, Jancis. *Vines, Grapes and Wines.* New York: Alfred A. Knopf, 1986.

Schoonmaker, Frank & Saint Roche, Christian R., Trad Frénois, Alain & Wilquin, Luce & Baudoux, Marc. *Le Guide Marabout des Vins de France et du Monde Entier.* Verviers, Belgique: Marabout, 1981.

Stevenson, Tom. *Sotheby's World Wine Encyclopedia.* Scarborough, Ontario: Prentice-Hall Canada Inc, 1988.

Underhill, James E. (Ted). *Making Better Wines.* A comprehensive manual for home winemaking at an intermediate level. Victoria, British Columbia: James E. (Ted) Underhill, 1990.

Wagner, M. Philip. *Grapes into Wine.* New York: Alfred A. Knopf, 1987.

Walker, Larry. "The Larry Walker Page," *Wine and Spirit International.* Teddington, Middlesex, Great Britain: August 1990.

Index

Index